NEW REVISED EDITION

PRESBYTERIAN WORSHIP
Its Meaning and Method

DONALD MACLEOD

John Knox Press
ATLANTA

To
Anne and Leslie
"daughters of my house and heart" (Byron)

Unless otherwise stated, Scripture quotations are from the Revised Standard Version, copyright 1946 and 1952 by the Division of Christian Education of the National Council of the Churches of Christ in the United States of America.

The prayer by Frank Colquhoun is reprinted by permission of Hodder & Stoughton Limited from *Contemporary Parish Prayers*. New material copyright © 1975 by Frank Colquhoun. First printed 1975. All rights reserved.

Library of Congress Cataloging in Publication Data

Macleod, Donald, 1913-
  Presbyterian worship.

  Bibliography: p.
  1. Liturgies—Presbyterian Church.   2. Presbyterian
Church. 3. Public worship.   I. Title.
BX9185.M23   1981   264'.05   80-82226
ISBN 0-8042-1813-7

© copyright M. E. Bratcher, 1965 and John Knox Press, 1980
10 9 8 7 6 5 4 3 2 1
Printed in the United States of America
John Knox Press
Atlanta, Georgia 30365

FOREWORD

This book is the author's modest response to the pressure of several needs; some of these are general and have been long felt, while others are more immediate and timely. The first is bibliographical. As a teacher of worship in a confessional school, it has been difficult to prescribe basic student readings that were not a mosaic of scattered assignments in a score of books, some of them rather expensive, others out of print. Apart from C. W. Baird's *Presbyterian Liturgies* (published originally in 1855), there was no one volume that was solely denominational, and none at all that combined liturgical theory *and* practice. Books on worship have been substantial both in numbers and scholarship, but many of them were written to embrace or please numerous traditions and therefore are unsatisfactory tools when a class of theological students has to be instructed in those emphases and practices that are peculiarly their own.

A second need is closely related to the first because it is more strictly professional. A lecturer can present in the classroom in a formal way those biblical and theological ideas that give meaning to worship, but monologues on the methods, techniques, and procedures of liturgical practice do not excite the student mind, especially when separated from the parish situation or handled without even a laboratory context. It is hoped that these pages will provide preparatory reading for seminar discussions later.

The third and chief reason for these chapters is to supply a need associated more specifically with the contemporary parish. This is the place where the most important work in the world is being done. At this basic level the life of the church is renewed, and the vigor of this renewal originates in the integrity and meaningfulness of its worship. Concurrently with the past several decades of revived interest in the liturgy of the Reformed tradition, two documents have been published which are bound to have considerable influence upon the worship and work of Presbyterian churches: *The Directory for Worship* (United Presbyterian Church, U.S.A.) and *The Directory for the Worship and Work of the Church* (Presbyterian Church, U.S.). Both treatises are well structured and are the products of careful thought and scholarly research. Moreover, with the appearance in 1972 of *The Worshipbook* (a joint enterprise among several branches of Presbyterianism), which has taken its place beside other service books including *The Book of Common Worship* (a classic in its own right), the liturgical resources of our Presbyterian tradition in America have been enriched and enlarged. By the many letters of inquiry which come in regularly, one cannot help being convinced that Presbyterian ministers are eager to follow intelligently the leading of their denomination. For these clergy in parish life this book is intended to be both a source of encouragement and a handy guide.

Our discussion begins with the problem of meaning as being basic to the whole worship experience in which we are involved. This is the central thrust of the first chapter. The succeeding chapters present this meaning at work in the usual worship occasions and responsibilities in which any average minister is called to lead and/or officiate. The author has drawn upon his own experience as a national missionary for four summers in Canada, as a small town minister, and later as a member of the staff of a large and influential city church. In each of these situations I was the proverbial learner and a seeker for answers to questions each unusual situation presented. The most recent tutor, however, has been the classroom queries, the honest contradictions, and the good incentive provided through the years by young theological students whose ministries are now bearing fruit in America and abroad. These pages provide more reflective and leisurely answers than the classroom period affords.

Considerable care has been taken to use inclusive language in the choice of pronouns referring to ministers, even at the cost of occasionally forfeiting some elegances of English style. In the matter of quotations, however, no alterations are made in any author's original composition.

The author is indebted to a host of exemplary ministers of the gospel, from whose inspiration and leadership in worship successive congregations have learned the faith and have been nurtured by it. This, however, does not exclude the many ideas from other minds that have influenced and shaped these chapters. As far as possible, appropriate credit is given and indebtedness acknowledged. Special appreciation is expressed to the director and staff of John Knox Press for their interest and competent services; to Mrs. Gretchen Thatcher, my secretary, who typed carefully the revisions of the pages of the 1965 edition; and to Mr. Thomas J. Pastuszka, an undergraduate, who read the proofs. It is the author's hope that through the sharing of helpful ideas our common worship will become truly a reciprocal exchange between the Creator and his creatures, between God and us.

Donald Macleod
Princeton Theological Seminary, Princeton, New Jersey

CONTENTS

1
Meaning in Worship

John Huxtable once said, "Christian worship is a dialogue between God and his people."[1] He was right in specifying that worship involves properly a two-way exchange between us and our Creator. *God acts—we respond.*[2] But any definition of worship remains incomplete unless the nature of what is done and of those who perform it is articulated clearly. For this reason Richard Davidson's definition is fuller in its meaning and implications: "Common worship is what we say and what we do when we stand together before God, realizing in high degree who he is and who we are."[3] Here are indicated some of the main elements of Christian worship. "What we say and what we do" denotes a corporate act. "Stand together before God" suggests not merely a place, but an event, a decisive confrontation or encounter with Deity. "Who He is" refers to the nature of God whose supreme worth is recognized and acknowledged. "Who we are" calls attention to our human nature and to the need within us that cries out to God for help.

It must be clear, however, that none of these ingredients comprising an act of Christian worship is probable or conceivable without belief; indeed "The core of worship is belief."[4] In *The Directory for Worship* the emphasis is similar: "Christian worship is ... a corporate response by the Church to God's mighty act of redemption in Jesus Christ."[5] Our worship then is the outcome of belief in a God who has done something for us and our salvation, and the shape of the liturgical act is determined by the nature of the divine work and of our response to it. What we say and what we do therefore on these high occasions will not be whole, nor ever have unity and meaning, if our basic beliefs are biased, short-sighted, or fragmentary. Moreover, the efficacy and quality of our response depends upon the activity in us of the Holy Spirit; for this reason the preparation for worship as individuals in private and as a congregation gathered to hear and receive God's Word will always be of singular importance.

Through a rethinking of our Protestant beliefs, particularly since World War II, and from seeing more clearly their relationship to worship, a fresh and vital interest in liturgical studies has been awakened among us. It will be useful to review at this point some of the major events and processes in order to keep this study within a proper perspective.

Some decades ago, William Temple, in his consecration address as archbishop of Canterbury, referred to the ecumenical movement as "the great new fact of our time." He was seeing with satisfaction the beginning of the end of the fragmented nature of the church within the context of what was coming rapidly to be understood as "one world." Were he alive today he might name liturgical concern as another great new fact, particularly among that part of the Reformed family known as Presbyterian. This phenomenon has been marked by various labels, but most of them are either inaccurate or clearly wrong. We hear, for example, of a general "liturgical revival" among Protestant churches and even of a "liturgical thaw" among Roman Catholics. But such descriptive phrases are usually less than accurate, because they give the impression with regard to the Reformed churches that there was a time when worship was carried on without a liturgy; that suddenly it was discovered that in order to worship God adequately certain machinery had to be retrieved or put into motion once again, and therefore liturgy was invented or revived as the appropriate vehicle.

Such thinking is nonsense. Indeed it appears all the more ridiculous when we examine the origin of the word "liturgy." It comes from the Greek *leiturgia,* meaning "the work or service of the people." Or, as Vilmos Vajta put it, "The liturgy is the form in which the congregation receives God's word in word and sacrament, and in which it, at the same time, clothes its prayers, its praise, and its confession of faith."⁶ It is not therefore the creation of any one person, but it is the activity and the product of the belief of that body of which Christ himself is the Head. And hence on Sunday mornings in every service of worship from Gothic cathedral to simple meeting house, the people's response is a liturgical act. Some may have an appointed liturgy, while others may be completely "on their own"; but the issue in Presbyterian churches is not, nor can it ever be, a matter of a liturgical *versus* a non-liturgical service. The problem has been *bad* liturgy—shapeless and formless—and the search for proper means by which it could be reformed and improved. In view of this, it can be said that there is no revival of liturgy as such today, but there is definitely a new climate of concern in which certain basic theological beliefs and emphases which were recognized or shaped as far back as the Reformation are being permitted to exercise their appropriate influence in and upon liturgical expression.

Naturally no one would venture to date the beginning of this rebirth of liturgical concern or to declare that on such-and-such a day certain new emphases appeared or some old ones were recaptured. Even a cursory review of our heritage of doctrine and tradition from the early church through the Reformation to the present day would indicate that the current has been fed by numerous smaller streams. However, since World War II there have been definite factors which have impinged upon the church—including ministers and congregations, jointly and separately—and have contributed to this pronounced desire to reform and inform our worship and to make the Sunday morning hour in the sanctuary a more meaningful encounter and dialogue with God.

The first person to have become involved in this new liturgical concern has been the minister. There was a time not too far past when any move on the part of a Presbyterian minister to adopt or champion a prescribed act of worship would be greeted with suspicion or stigmatized as a sign of "going high church." Or, as Massey Shepherd described it, "going over,

piece by piece, to Liberalism and Ritualism." But such would
not be the opinion today, except among representatives of the
closed mind or of some cult of ecclesiastical negativism. Today the ministry lives in a new climate. The winds of change
have been blowing from fresh regions of Christian thought.
Pivotal minds and their books have shocked ministers out of
their pastoral complacency and liturgical stagnation where, as
one minister put it, they had become "rutted in." Indeed the
clergy's stature among lay leaders would become suspect
very quickly were their minds not to show a growing edge
that is sharpened by contemporary movements in religious
thoughts.

Some of these influences began in germ form decades ago
with Rudolf Otto's *Idea of the Holy*, with his emphasis upon
the *other-ness* of the unseen and the need for a proper balance between subjectivity and objectivity in our approach to
God. Other influences came with the new concept of the
unity of the Bible and the evidences of the influence of the
Old Testament upon the New, the relationship of the Jewish
liturgical cult to the Christian, and the continuity of the covenant of grace that finds its symbolic expression in the Christian sacraments, as explored by such able scholars as Oscar
Cullmann, Gilbert Cope, and Eduard Schweizer. Nor at this
point can the whole christological emphasis be overlooked,
with its exploration of Calvin's idea of "union with Christ" as
"the chief end of the whole mystery of the Lord's Supper," its
rediscovery of the meaning for worship of "through Jesus
Christ our Lord," and the new insights into the concept of the
presence of Christ in the sacraments, in studies made by Joachim Jeremias, Max Thurian, and Richard Paquier. But chiefly has the new stimulus come from the modern ferment in
biblical theology generally associated with the monumental
writings of Karl Barth. No one can accept the Barthian concept of revelation in which "the Word of God is God himself,
communicating himself and giving himself to us"[7] and not
feel and see its implications for worship and preaching.
These are merely some of the movements that have created

this new climate from which no minister has been able to remain isolated and through which intimations of the renewal of the church have been seen. The second group involved here is the congregation, for whom and to whom the preacher is responsible. This group has not been inactive. Indeed these people are no longer a traditionally passive entity, but are a challenge to whomsoever their pastoral oversight has been entrusted. It is true they move and live weekly on levels and in areas of culture with other than a Christian frame of reference, and often for some of them the time given to Christian worship, either public or private, is fractional and intermittent. Nevertheless the discipline and the quality of their experiences—whatever they be—in the areas of science, government, music, and the arts, have created minds that refuse to accept "just anything" in the name of religion on the Lord's Day. If the minister thinks differently about them or has underestimated their liturgical appreciation and perception, he or she has misjudged them. A layman from the Province of Manitoba, Canada, wrote plainly:

A good many church families and ministers seem to feel that the only way to keep the Church going is a constant round of meetings, as if it depended solely upon organization. By far the great majority of our people are seeking desperately for a real faith in God, but it is easy to become so busy that we can't hear what God is trying to say to us.[8]

It ought to come as no surprise then that beneath the bulging statistics and complex organizational character of the modern congregation, there is an earnest desire among Christian men and women to have a share in the community of faith that praises God for his glory and serves them in life. The minister therefore will have to take the initiative in articulating the objectives of the Christian community, and he or she can show the way primarily through worship. But it must be worship that has meaning; otherwise the revolutionary role of the church will be lost among the minor details of secular or social services.

I

In view of this challenge to the church and its ministry, the logical query is: where do we go from here? If the worship of the church is to have unity, shape, and relevance to human need, it must have meaning. But the way to meaning is not through the methods of either of two contemporary groups, the ritualists or the aesthetes. Ritual and liturgy, it must be said, are not synonymous. Ritual is composed of the words of the service of worship, while liturgy is the corporate activity in which the people engage. Some leaders of worship think that the service is enriched and given deeper meaning simply through patching up a prescribed order, by adding here and there a few responses by the choir, or by cramming the hour with fragments of unrelated canticles and responses from the early church. The end result is usually length and breadth, but no depth. Then there are the eager aesthetes who separate unconsciously the holiness of beauty from the beauty of holiness. For them worship becomes entirely a matter of the senses and of psychological impression. Their yardstick is sentiment, which can slip very quickly into sentimentality and can range all the way from what is dainty to what is maudlin. The common fault of both of these groups is a failure to realize that the *whole* person is involved in worship and that love to God embraces in balanced proportion the heart, mind, and will.

The search for meaning, then, is the handle by which the contemporary revival of interest in worship is to be grasped and the most useful direction of this new concern determined. This is crucial because it has to do with even the *raison d'être* of the church itself. The church's mission is to the whole person; and the crowning expression of it will be in the response it receives from the call, "I appeal to you therefore, brethren, by the mercies of God, to present your bodies as a living sacrifice, holy and acceptable to God, which is your spiritual worship."[9] Such worship is concerned with every aspect of our being, and hence the church today faces here a compelling challenge which it must neither miss nor fail. Only as the church inserts meaning into its worship and thereby projects or supplies a structure and framework for our common life can it hope to make us realize the peace and power of God as living realities. On the other hand, without the reconciling thrust of such meaning into community life, the church will not likely save for good a generation which has to move continually in this contemporary atmosphere of materialism, fear, and downright paganism.

The first step in any attempt to secure meaning in worship is to discern clearly those theological presuppositions that are inherent in a distinctively Christian liturgical act.

Lutherans begin worship with the words "In the name of the Father, and of the Son, and of the Holy Ghost," which is a recognition that worship must always heed definite theological presuppositions and, equally important, be under the judgment of theology. What we believe about God is the corrective of what we do. As Neville Clark has said, "What is believed will and must govern what is done in worship."[10] What is more, since God is who he is and we are what we are, each periodic encounter with him in worship makes us feel anew the decision of the Eternal upon us and what he did to effect our reconciliation.

It is clear then that no authentic reform in worship can happen unless the changes that are made are primarily theologically oriented and unless those who make them are theologically informed. Theology is grounded in a revelation. This revelation, moreover, is a self-disclosure of God. It cannot be, therefore, a matter of our rising or reaching by our own efforts to grasp it; it is the invasion into our helpless life and consciousness of his presence and purpose. If then, as Davidson states further, "our words and actions will depend on what He is like before whom we stand,"[11] mere definitions of God will not be sufficient. The classic statement from *The Westminster Shorter Catechism* is: "God is a Spirit, infinite, eternal, and unchangeable, in his being, wisdom, power, holiness, justice, goodness, and truth." But originally the New Testament was more personal: "He who has seen me has seen the Father"(John 14:9). It was in and through Christ people learned supremely what God is like. Jesus was "the Word made flesh." This was a presentation of God in a person. But we cannot stop even there. We must acknowledge that ours is a Triune God. This we tend to forget, and this omission has been the means of causing much imbalance in Christian worship. For, when the emphasis is placed upon God's soverignty alone and upon his word of righteousness and judgment, it is very easy for worship to feature exclusively God's demand and consequently become didactic, hortatory, and for the most part, intellectual. On the other hand, when the proclamation of God's Word is slighted, the act of worship lacks a constitutive element, and through an overemphasis upon devotion, it can release the worshipers from the claim of a higher obedience and leave them to lose themselves in private contemplation of the mystical presence of our Lord. Also, if the role of the Holy Spirit in worship is not recognized fully or is poorly understood, the fellowship of the sanctuary can become little more than a jolly get-together perpetuated by habit or institutionalism or maybe an experience of a weird numinous feeling whose subjectivity and introversion dissolve the objective reality of God.

We see now how very responsible to certain theological presuppositions our liturgical renewal must be today. For if our worship is to have meaning, shape, and unity, we must recognize a downward movement of the Word of God, becoming real in Jesus Christ, and an upward movement of our response, with the Holy Spirit bringing forth new creations from this tremendous encounter in the realm of grace and faith. Indeed our worship must be the expression of this gospel, and in devotion of this kind the church will discover its real mission. No words sum up this section better than those of Neville Clark:

The God we adore is Blessed Trinity, Father, Son and Holy Spirit . . . The worship of a God like that must ever be Trinitarian in tone, Christological in pattern, centred [sic] on Word and Sacrament; corporate, congregational, embodied; awesome, exultant, ordered, and free.[12]

Second, we must recognize the priority worship holds in the life of the church.

Now the word "priority" implies primacy among emphases or concerns, but in the case of the Christian church, it suggests a primacy among its responsible acts. Therefore when we speak of the priority of worship, the implication is that here lies the church's basic activity. Indeed it has been asserted again and again that worship is the only indispensable activity of the Christian church. Massey Shepherd writes, "The ordering and conduct of worship is the one distinctive and essential task of the Church.[13] Thirty-five years earlier, Dean Sperry of Harvard said:

This (ordering and conduct of worship) is central and inalienable.

So long as the church bids men to the worship of God and provides a simple and credible vehicle for worship it need not question its place, mission, and influence in the world. If it loses faith in the act of worship, is thoughtless in the ordering of worship, and careless in the conduct of worship, it need not look to its avocations to save it. It is dead at its heart, and no chafing of the extremities . . . will bring back the life that has left it.[14]

Now, what is the basis for this claim? Actually it is that initially the church came into being in worship. Moreover, in the constant program of meaningful acts of worship its life is nourished and sustained. As men and women gather in fellowship to acknowledge their frail humanity as they can do nowhere else, as they hear declared to them God's Word by which God claims them as his own, as they give thanks to God for his gift in Jesus Christ by which they are made into what they ought to be, and as they surrender and offer themselves to become instruments in his hands to do his will—here the church begins and, in times of spiritual poverty, reconstitutes its very being. "Thy kingdom come" is the prayer of the church in all ages, but it is preceded by "Our Father who art in heaven, Hallowed be thy name." The worship of God is primary and is that dramatization of the faith that makes the kingdom possible.

Worship then is the high occasion when an external expression of the faith of the church is made. Luther said, "To have a God is to worship God." It is here and not in our creeds that the deepest expression of the church's faith appears. The creed is but the formulation of that to which worship witnesses and testifies. Worship, however, is the living form of faith and involves the whole church as well as the whole person. Moreover, it is in this act we see the witness of the church at its finest, and it is from this act that the devotion of individual Christians receives its nourishment. This is the center from which all other actions of the church take their meaning.

But what about all those unstructured, pointless, and emotionally disoriented services of worship in Protestant churches? This has been one of the major reasons why the faith of the church has not been proclaimed and why Alfred R. Shands quotes Theodore Wedel as saying, "Biblical Christianity . . . is an unknown religion today for the vast majority."[15] So many of our services, Dr. Rinderknecht of Zürich says, "are strange and incomprehensible to the outsider."[16] But whenever God's voice speaks to the church in word and sacrament, it is not only a call to faith but also a call to witness to the new life of faith. Here the service of the church begins. In the early church, worship was the vital center from which a new spirit moved and regulated the life of the Christian community. This could not have been possible if it were only a matter of the church's coming together at a set time and performing a series of things willy-nilly in a particular place. Indeed, in the New Testament the word *ecclesia* can refer generally to "an orderly meeting of citizens," but what distinguished the church from such gatherings was that it came "together in the name of Jesus." And "togetherness" was never the automatic consequence of merely assembling in one place; their "worship was above all the Body of Christ taking visible form."[17] Moreover, it was from such a wholesome experience that the early church went out to change the world. Hence the church in the twentieth century must re-establish the priority of this type of worship—worship that reflects the peculiar genius of its faith—if it is to realize its mission and if through its members the Holy Spirit is to "permeate and influence the world, to make them the salt of the earth, and to make the disciples of the Lord realize that this is what they are."[18]

Further, in many discussions of Reformed worship there has been a tendency to overlook the significance of tradition. Frequently we are dubbed a group without a liturgical heritage or a continuity of meaning in what we do. Luther and Calvin, it is true, did not set out to form a new church. Their aim was the reformation of the one they were in. But when the Roman Catholic Church refused to acknowledge and rectify its abuses and faults, the Reformers broke with it and tried to recapture the ancient traditions of the early church. Their hope then was, as David H. C. Read has said, "the purging rather than the destroying of a tradition." And the fresh tradition they initiated and the processes they launched were not peripheral changes, but could be traced to radical reorientations in the sphere of faith.

Now we of the twentieth century, in view of the meaninglessness of so much of our worship, dare not begin *de novo* with liturgical reform. Already we see that too much "freewheeling" has produced two unrealistic groups, the experimenters and innovators, on the one hand, who are devotees of colored lights, pastel shades, and "mood building"; and, on the other hand, the "hidebound" traditionalists who adhere blindly to the axiom of custom: it has always been done this way here. They are marked by the "antiquarian spirit" and the "museum mind." Tradition, however, is never a dead thing; if it is worth anything, it is a living reality. It cannot be otherwise if the Holy Spirit is at work in the church. As Presbyterians, for example, we should never feel that only the Roman Catholics, Eastern Orthodox, and Anglicans have all the precedents to which our references and appeals must be made. Our theological presuppositions are written into the faith of Christendom. In our act of worship we have a liturgical tradition of richness and quality and a shape derived from a rethinking of the faith the Reformers received.

John Calvin, on the title page of his liturgy, wrote *"Forme of Prayers and Administration of the Sacraments According to the Custom of the Ancient Church."* W. D. Maxwell has put all forever in his debt by tracing both John Knox's *Genevan Service Book* and Calvin's *Forme of Prayers* back to their common source in Diebold Schwarz's German Mass, celebrated on February 16, 1524, in St. John's Chapel of the Cathedral of St. Lawrence, Strasbourg. From this process it is apparent that our liturgy is catholic in origin while remaining evangelical in spirit. What the Reformers removed were all references and prayers to saints, the Virgin, the Mass as a sacrifice. Then in the language of the people and for the sake of the people, they gave them back a service that was a corporate communion. After Schwarz came Martin Bucer under whom the sermon emerged into a fuller place, ceremonial was curbed, and the congregation was given a larger part in the services, particularly with the singing of Psalms and hymns. This was the liturgy Calvin borrowed and simplified during his sojourn in Strasbourg (1538–1541) and introduced later in Geneva. Now it was not Calvin's intention, for example, to replace sacramental worship by a preaching service. His aim was twofold: to restore the communion to its primitive simplicity and proper proportions as a weekly service, and within this service to give the Holy Scriptures their authoritative place. The corporate worship of the early church was his fond hope. For him, to the liturgy of the Word must be added the liturgy of the Upper Room. As Maxwell has said, "To Calvin the 'means of grace' were twofold, consisting of *both* the Word and the Sacraments. The Ministry was a ministry of the Word *and* the Sacraments."[19]

Here we see that the reformation under Calvin was both constructive and conservative. It was intended to cleanse the liturgy from all the superstition of medieval times and to restore the simplicity, purity, and adequacy of the worship of the undivided church. And to us he has given the heritage of an act of worship that is *Soli Deo Gloria*: God is sovereign and all our worship is to his glory. This gives to our worship its objective character, but at the same time it lays a demand upon the worshiper. There was more, however: the Bible became the norm, and according to its spirit our worship would always be judged; the Word of God read and preached became the indispensable and initiatory thrust of the act of worship and the dynamic principle of the church's life; and the congregation's response to this declaration of the Word—in prayer, praise, sacrament, in short, in faith—completes the dialogue of the sanctuary in which the whole Christian community rises to its new status as the Body of Christ, "chosen by God and for God." Calvinistic worship has been criticized as bare and unimaginative, with little drama and with less devotional than intellectual appeal, but, as D. H. Hislop has said, it is unexcelled as "an illustration of the type of worship founded exclusively on the idea of revelation." Doumergue's estimate is both clear and fair:

> All the essential elements of worship were there. And perhaps not less important they were united in an organism that was very simple, yet supple and strong. Calvin is, in fact, of all the Reformers the one who most steadfastly rejected the division of worship into two parts. . . .The Calvinian cultus is one.[20]

II

What we have been saying thus far accords with Eduard Thurneysen's remark that "in her worship we find the heart of the Church, without which her life would quickly wither away."[21] But it is not enough to say that worship has priority in the church's life and that in order to be meaningful, theology, tradition, and faith must be involved. We need to explore now two practical implications which meaningful worship has for the mission and witness of the church, especially for that renewal which is felt to be so urgent.

A. When the act of worship has meaning, it will assume an authentic shape. Recently, while talking with the pulpit nominating committee of a congregation, someone remarked about the lack of any norm for Presbyterian worship. Another added that during the committee's visitation of a score of churches, in no two Presbyterian services were the orders of worship similar in arrangement and form. And what was equally puzzling: rarely could the members—indeed not even the minister—provide a rationale for the series of things that were said and done in the stated hour. This is disturbing; indeed, it is appalling. It is nothing less than an unconscious flouting of all the theological, biblical, historical, and psychological factors out of which an authentic act of Christian worship is made. On the other hand, whenever the integrity of these elements as a whole is taken properly into account, something substantial takes shape, and this shape is authentic to the degree that the act of worship has theological meaning that can be both defended and explained.

A meaningful service of worship in a Presbyterian church will consist of the preparation or approach[22] and two main movements: the Proclamation of the Word and the Fellowship of Prayer. (Calvin's *The Forme of Prayers* has these two main movements: The Liturgy of the Word and The Liturgy of the Upper Room.) History points to this format as early as the second century as the essential liturgical framework that continued down to the Reformation. Indeed the Divine Liturgy of the Eastern Orthodox Church and the Mass of the Roman Catholic Church consists merely of elaborations upon this basic structure. As Richard Davidson once remarked, "The Church in its infancy wrought out an action in two stages [Liturgy of the Word and Liturgy of the Upper Room]; this action is for all ages the norm of Christian worship."[23] And this action took its shape from the simple principle that "worship depends upon revelation; and Christian worship is the Church's response to the whole *biblical* revelation."[24]

(1) *The Preparation:* No one is ready for the high experience of public worship. For the preacher too, it can be, and indeed should be, a solemn responsibility. The people who are about to present themselves before God may ask: who and what are we?

Arthur John Gossip once described in these words the modern complexion of things:

> What a poor way of life ours is, huddled into the jostling traffic of our narrow streets, and penned between the crowding houses; and above us only the twinkling of electric signs, and the loud pushfulness of blatant advertisements about little nothings; and never a glimpse of the wide spaces of the heavens, and the awe, and the majesty, and the calm, of the eternal stars.[25]

They are little more than a miscellaneous group of earthy persons who come into the sanctuary from their fragmented ways, who are beset by diverse interests and passions, and who are to be welded together by a common spiritual experience into the Body of Christ.

The service begins with the Call to Worship which takes the place of the bell in the Roman Mass. The people are stilled as they hear the words "Let us worship God." This declaration pulls aside the veil and as the people respond in the words of an appropriate objective hymn about the nature or attributes of God, the majesty of the Eternal is unfolded before them. Calvin said that the first thing in religion is the proper adoration of God; *The Westminster Shorter Catechism* declares, "Man's chief end is to glorify God, and to enjoy him forever." The hymn delineates for them the face of God and as a consequence they are drawn by the Prayer of Adoration into the objectivity of worship. The hymn recognizes God as God; the Prayer of Adoration gives glory that is due unto his name. Incidentally, to open a service with only a prayer of invocation, as is done by many pietistic and holiness sects, is to begin by focusing upon ourselves and not upon the being of God. It is a look at self in the light of self and not in the light of God. In his constructive little book, *Concerning Worship*, W. D. Maxwell has this appropriate comment: "A prayer of invocation should not be substituted for the prayer of adoration, for adoration is primary."[26]

Then follows the Prayer of Confession. When the people see who God is, they are led to see what they are themselves. As Augustine said in his *Confessions*, "I was dragged up to Thee by Thy beauty, but dragged back again by my own weight." They confess their sense of sinfulness and conclude it with a plea for help in their time of need. The Assurance of Pardon follows, in which the minister declares the divine *forgivingness* of God toward every believer. What is more fitting now than a song of praise? The Preparation ends with the whole congregation, singing, for example, Isaac Watts' great hymn to the tune of Old Hundredth:

From all that dwell below the skies
Let the Creator's praise arise:
Let the Redeemer's name be sung
Through every land, in every tongue.

Eternal are Thy mercies, Lord;
Eternal truth attends Thy word:
Thy praise shall sound from shore to shore,
Till suns shall rise and set no more.

It should be noted also that at this point Calvin left the communion table, from where the first part of the service was conducted, and went to the pulpit for the *"lecture et explication de L'evangile*—the reading and explication of the Gospel."[27]

(2) *The Proclamation of the Word:* Members of the Reformed tradition are a people of a book, and that book is central and fundamental to the life of every congregation. Since worship presupposes a revelation and since, as *The Directory of Worship*[28] states, "Scripture is the record of God's mighty acts in making himself known to [people], and is also a means by which, through the power of the Holy Spirit, God makes himself known to [people] today," therefore "public worship will always include the reading and hearing of the written

Word of God." "Proclamation," says Eduard Schweizer, "is the heart of worship."[29] (Incidentally, a Psalm read responsively is not an Old Testament Lesson; originally and quite properly the Psalm was an act of praise.) There should be both Old and New Testament Lessons[30] separated by the Gloria Patri.[31] The New Testament Lesson points to the fulfillment of God's revelation begun by the record of the Old Testament. Here is a fitting place for an anthem when the choir, singing alone, represents the congregation.[32] The sermon follows as the actualization of the Word. Or, as John Marsh put it, "[In the sermon] the Word which God spoke in his historic actions is intended to come to contemporaneous effectiveness."[33] Then the congregation affirms its faith in the words of the Apostles' Creed.[34] The people proceed to the Sacrament (if it is to be celebrated on this occasion).

(3) *The Fellowship of Prayer:* Charles Cuthbert Hall in an essay on worship wrote, "The Divine giving is, in the Christian scheme of worship, the inspiration of the human giving."[35] In other words, having seen a vision—through the reading, hearing, and preaching of the Word—of the God of all grace and what he has done for us, the early church brought in its gifts of bread and wine, i.e., an Offertory took place. These people believed there could be no worship without sacrifice. God *gave* for them; they in a symbolic way respond with their substance—their gifts as symbols of their devotion, toil, and sacrifice.

Then comes the Prayer of Thanksgiving in which the people are reminded of all the good things they have received, but at the same time, aware of being part of the great family of God, they think of their kindred and go on into the Prayer of Intercession. In these intercessions, however, they still offer themselves to God to become the medium through which these blessings will be implemented for others. This is their dedication; its substructure is the faith they have in the Word and promise of God. To quote Cuthbert Hall again, "Worship is the expression and the action of faith, and faith is the root and the motive of worship."[36] The Lord's Prayer follows.

Here they gather up all their prayers said and unsaid in the words of their Lord. Here they identify themselves with him "who ever maketh intercession" for all people. Dom Gregory Dix's comment is appropriate here:

> In all christian churches from the earliest moment at which we have definite evidence the prayers were universally placed last, after the sermon, and have remained there ever since. This was evidently a fixed christian tradition ... to be so universal and firm on the point.[37]

The concluding hymn may continue the note of thanksgiving or it may remind the people of the responsibility the intercessions and petitions imply and entail. With the hymn ended, the Benediction is given. It is interesting to notice that at the close of the Jewish fellowship meal out of which the framework of the Sacrament of the Lord's Supper emerged, the leader lifted his hand in blessing: "The Lord bless you and keep you. . . ."

The foregoing act of worship is generally known as "Ante-Communion," i.e., the Service of Holy Communion to the end of the intercessions, without consecration and communion. The Directory for Worship urges more frequent celebration of the Sacrament of the Lord's Supper by pointing out that such is "integral to the full ordering of public worship."[38] Many congregations, where at one time only a quarterly observance was customary, have now as many as eight opportunities (which includes a Maundy Thursday service) when this sacrament is celebrated. (The discussion of this fuller service will be taken up in Section II of Chapter 4.)

B. If the act of worship has meaning, it will emerge in a way of life. The service is now concluded and the people go out into the world of the many, but they go out as one in Christ; they are his Body. Once Forsyth said about the role of the minister: "He is to preach to the Church from the Gospel so that with the Church he may preach the Gospel to the world."[39] And equally important, the shape of the act of worship must become the pattern for everyday life.

From what has been said thus far, it is clear that if a new way of life is to be initiated, it must begin in the worship of the church, in the fellowship of that community of persons where praise, confession, testimony, and dedication are sincerely made. The worshiping group is a living, organic body that must move out into the life of the world and redeem it from the inside. The obedience pledged in the sanctuary has to be carried into the activities of the daily program. The prayer of St. Richard of Chichester sums up the need:

... that we may *know* thee more clearly; *love* thee more dearly; and *follow* thee more nearly day by day.

Worship and life belong together. Separation spells sterility for one and impoverishment for the other. George Mac-Leod has said, "The ultimate worship of God is what we do in the realm of service and obedience in the market place." And C. F. D. Moule has cautioned us that worship becomes "meaningless and barren unless it issues in life and work." In the sense that worship is intended for God's glory alone, it is an end in itself; but like every human encounter with the Unseen it has inevitable by-products and corollaries that are significant in and indeed saviors of life. If there were not, then the whole relevance of worship to life would be destroyed and religion would not appear to have to do with the redemption of men's bodies along with their souls. As long as worship has meaning—that is, as long as it has an object in God, is a shared experience in Christ, and by the help of the Holy Spirit calls forth an act of faith—then it will have a shape and a claim that will embrace and eventually change the character of our common life. William Temple once said, "This world can be saved from political chaos and collapse by one thing only, and this is worship."[40] The shape of that worship, as we have seen, results simply from a Word of redemption declared and the congregation's response and surrender to it. But this Word by its very intensity implies extensity. When people hear it and accept it, they are carried by its moving contagion out into society, and then others are drawn by its

presence and claim and they offer their labor, their posses-
sions, and their abilities for the fullest use in the realm of
God. The form of worship becomes then the shape of our
common existence also, namely, God ever speaking to us, and
our returning an adoring response. This response involves offering; it implies sacrifice. According to an age-old practice,
we bring our gifts of bread and wine—the symbols of all of
life—and God gives them back to us to nurture us so that we
will be spiritually competent to do his holy Will. All life becomes a partnership with God; the preacher and the church
make up the living organic community, serving as co-workers
with their sovereign Lord in his plan for the redemption of
the world.

LITERATURE

Brenner, S.F. *The Way of Worship*. New York: Macmillan Co., 1944.
Herbert, A.S. *Worship in Ancient Israel*, Ecumenical Studies in
    Worship, No.#5. Richmond: John Knox Press, 1959.
Hislop, D.H. *Our Heritage in Public Worship*. Edinburgh: T. & T.
    Clark, 1935.
Macdonald, A.B. *Christian Worship in the Primitive Church*. New
    York: Scribner's, 1934.
Maxwell, W.D. *An Outline of Christian Worship*. London: Oxford
    University Press, 1958.
McMillan, William. *The Worship of the Scottish Reformed Church,
    1550–1638*. Glasgow: University of Glasgow, 1930.
Micklem, Nathaniel (ed.). *Christian Worship*. Oxford: The Claren-
    don Press, 1936.
Moule, C.F.D. *Worship in the New Testament Church*, Ecumenical
    Studies in Worship, No. 9. Richmond: John Knox Press, 1961.

2
The Act of Worship

A service of worship based upon the principles outlined in the foregoing chapter would assume the following shape.

WORSHIP

The Preparation

Organ Prelude	"Chorale in E Major"	César Franck
Call to Worship	("Let us worship God," followed by Scripture)	
Processional	"Praise ye the Lord"	Lobe Den Herren
Hymn No. 1		
Prayers:	Adoration (the people standing)	
	Confession (seated and in unison)	
	Assurance of Pardon	
Hymn of Praise	"From all that dwell below the skies"	
No. 33		Old Hundredth

The Proclamation of the Word

Prayer for Illumination	
Old Testament Lesson	Ezekiel 36:22–32
Gloria Patri	Old Scottish Chant
New Testament Lesson	1 Corinthians 13
Anthem "The King of Love My Shepherd Is"	Edward Bairstow
Sermon "The Pulse of Love"	1 John 3:14–17
Apostles' Creed	

The Fellowship of Prayer

Offering		
Anthem	"God so loved the world"	John Stainer
Dedication		
Prayers of Thanksgiving and Intercession		Lord's Prayer
Recessional	"O Love that wilt not let me go"	
Hymn No. 400		St. Margaret
Benediction	Choral Amen (choir and congregation)	
Organ Postlude	"Fugue in F Minor"	G. F. Handel

The above is an Order of Worship for those Sundays when the sacraments are not celebrated. The following discussion is a running commentary of explanation and instruction for each individual action.

I

About half an hour prior to the beginning of the service, the minister or a deacon should make a routine "check-up" of the sanctuary in order to be assured that everything is in readiness for the act of worship. There is no excuse for embarrassing incidents and situations that occur in many churches when hymnbooks removed from the pulpit or lectern have not been replaced, Bible markers remain twisted or carelessly crossed, seasonal changes of the antependia are overlooked, or unsightly arrangements of the flower baskets and stands have been allowed to remain. A responsible and sensitive sexton who takes pride in the things entrusted to his or her care can be a strong ally of the minister in these things, but unfortunately persons of this quality and devotion are still in a minority. Every aid of the minister in worship, such as hymnbooks, books of prayers, or bulletins, ought to be plainly in sight and readily accessible. Fumbling and infelicity in the pulpit can readily create uneasiness in the pew.

In some churches—and it is a salutary custom—members of the session meet with the minister in the vestry for a brief season of prayer prior to the service, led either by each one in a week-to-week rotation, or every Sunday in sentence prayers by as many as feel inclined. When the time to enter the sanctuary approaches (10:50 A.M., for example) both minister and choir should meet together in a regularly appointed room for a final briefing in any details of the service. A prayer, prepared and well thought out, should be offered within the hearing of the whole choir and ought never to be merely a feeble bleat in competition with the roar of the organ. This meeting should be unhurried and can do much to permit the choir to enter the sanctuary with a calm and relaxed disposition. Much is contributed to the quality of a service by a choir whose members approach their task of leading in praise with the realization that they have a significant and holy function to fulfill.

> O Thou who hast taught us to glorify Thee in our bodies and our spirits which are Thine: help us that whether we pray with our hearts, or listen with our minds, or make music with hands or voices—whatsoever we do in word or deed—we may do all in the Name of the Lord Jesus, giving thanks unto Thee through Him. Amen.[1]

or

> Bless, O God, those who sing in the choir of this church, that with heart and voice they may make melody to the Lord; and may they so lead our praises that together we may magnify your glorious name, through Jesus Christ our Savior.[2]

Before meeting with the choir, however, the minister will have prepared himself or herself for the high act of leading the people through worship into a meaningful experience of God's presence. Never should one permit the vestry to be overrun with chatty people on trivial errands which can press any person into distraction at a time when composure is essential. There is a point of time beyond which the vestry door should be shut and the minister left *alone* while a section of a Psalm or a selection from a devotional classic may be read meditatively and then, leaning upon the assurances of God's eternal grace, he or she may say:

> O Lord my God, without whom I can do nothing as I ought; go with me, I beseech Thee, into Thy House, and so guide me by Thy Holy Spirit that I may devoutly lead the worship of Thy people, worthily proclaim Thy Gospel, and shew forth Thy truth and grace to all who wait upon Thee; through Jesus Christ our Lord. Amen.[3]

or

> Prepare me, O God, for the worship of your house, and give me grace to serve you with reverence, joy, and thanksgiving; through Jesus Christ our Lord. Amen.[4]

The minister may proceed with the choir or may enter by the shortest route to the appropriate place in the sanctuary. Frequently this matter, is settled by the physical complexion or layout of the church, which may or may not be adequate or suitable, depending usually upon the financial resources of the congregation. A tactful minister, however, will use to the best advantage whatever resources or equipment the congregation has, until through careful planning something more appropriate can be secured. By whatever door he or she enters, one must appear as being aware of what is about to happen. One must be natural, divested of all superficial affectations, and untainted by the least mark of slovenliness. One may be solemn, yet without the dour countenance of the tomb; at all events the minister must wear the expression of one who is glad to go up to the house of the Lord.

THE PREPARATION

The Organ Prelude

This is not an adjunct or a filler while the people are coming in and being seated. It is part of the act of worship. It ought to be named in the bulletin, and if there are some historical facts of unusual interest about the music, a brief written notice may be included among the announcements. Moreover, every congregation should be informed as tactfully as possible that the organ prelude is a time for preparation for worship and should not be a period for exchanging pleasantries or evaluating millinery creations.

In his excellent book, *Steps Toward a Singing Church*, Donald D. Kettring describes his performance in the organ prelude as follows:

> THE SERVICE PRELUDE is scheduled for 10:45 [A.M.]. . . . Ideally, the first prelude number begins with quiet or medium organ, and rather soon reaches pretty full organ. Thus the people are not shocked with sudden full organ, yet are early commanded to listen. The last four minutes of prelude time are always quiet music, so that a hush tends to descend on the church.

If possible, in the selection of preludes, it is good to have some relationship of composer, theme, or period, between them and the anthems. The listed preludes come to a conclusion at 10:58 [A.M.], at which time the choir members are leaving the choir room (where the ministers have conducted devotions with them). . . .[5]

The Call to Worship

This act is no more or less than its name suggests and implies. It is a call to attention and is intended to "still" the people. "[It] takes the place of the 'bell' in the Roman services."[6] This end can be achieved more fully and readily if the congregation rises when the minister stands to speak. Selections should be made from the Bible and be said from memory. The minister should speak in the middle register and with moderate tempo. No appropriate mood or tone for the service is set by anyone who shouts the Call to Worship like a military sergeant or mumbles the lines incoherently. Variety of choice from week to week is essential and selections according to the various emphases of the Christian year will contribute to unity of theme in the service. A good Call to Worship appropriately declared can make the people both to be still and to know that God is God.[7]

The Processional Hymn

Whether or not this hymn is sung as a processional, its theme should assist the congregation to focus upon some attribute of God's Being. Such selections as Neander's "Praise ye the Lord, the Almighty, the King of creation," Watts' "Bless, O my soul! the living God," or Heber's "Holy, Holy, Holy! Lord God Almighty!" are great, objective hymns of adoration and praise. The Scottish Psalter, moreover, provides a wide variety of "noble vehicles of fellowship with God because they lift us out of ourselves, and out of the mood of our time, into a higher world, where all creatures look upward and rejoice in God."[8]

Now the processional method of entrance has something

to commend it. There is an impressive and moving factor involved in seeing a great choir enter the nave to the strains of a strong hymn of adoration. It appeals, for example, to those for whom the element of pageantry in worship has an attraction. There are times and places, however, when it should not be encouraged: in the church in which an awkward physical layout does not permit an orderly processional, or when the choristers are few, or where a crowded narthex creates added confusion. On the other hand, any unnatural or circuitous rerouting of singers is best not done at all. As Scott F. Brenner remarked, "This is no time for marching around the walls of Jericho or for the fanfare of figures on parade."[9] Other critics maintain that a processional rules out the use of many great hymns of praise because their tunes are written in tempos not suitable for this purpose and therefore their treasures are neglected.

This latter criticism, however, is valid only when the processional is "marched." The late Rupert Sircom of the Westminster Presbyterian Church, Minneapolis, gave a mature commentary on method when he wrote:

> The march has always been identified with secular life and its expression, and not with the spirit of the liturgy. A marching priest or chorister is in direct conflict with the spirit and content of all Christian liturgy. . . . Why then should a choir march into church, proclaiming its entrance as "performers," when we know that the choir is a leader in worship and not in musical performance for its own sake? . . . For those who seek Church music in Church, a march is not Church music at all, and surely is not considered good taste in worship.[10]

Von Ogden Vogt provides two couplets as explanation of the processional and recessional actions and emphasizes the elements of approach at the beginning of worship and of withdrawal and dedication at the close.

Processional: Up from the world of the many,
                    To the over-world of the One.

Recessional: Back to the world of the many
                    To fulfill the life of the One.

Each minister, however, must decide with the choir director the procedure that is most feasible in the local situation. Some may take sides—and not without justifiable reasons—with Henry Sloane Coffin's suggestion that clergy and choir enter by the shortest route and take their seats in silence, and as the prelude dies away the minister should rise to give the Call to Worship.

The Prayers of Adoration and Confession

As we indicated in Chapter 1, the Prayer of Adoration draws us into the objectivity of worship. The opening hymn recognizes God as God; the Prayer of Adoration gives glory that is due unto his name. Here the minister makes no petition, but in reverent and glad submission expresses the thought of the hymn writer who cried,

> O Lord of heaven and earth and sea,
> To Thee all praise and glory be;
> How shall we show our love to Thee
> Who givest all?
> —Christopher Wordsworth (1807–1885)

Week by week in the same pulpit will demand freshness and creativity on the part of the minister. Variety can be obtained from constant companionship with the Psalms, the great Christian hymns, and devotional writings of high and classic quality. Biblical phraseology is particularly helpful, but no prayer should be simply a string of scriptural phrases, nor should a minister wear any ascriptions threadbare. Moreover, a sense of awe and wonder should characterize and permeate this prayer, which cannot be the case if and when the minister's approach is marred by casual familiarity. With a simple "Let us pray," one may properly begin:

> Lord God eternal, holy, almighty, merciful; maker of all things by Thy power, ruler of all things in Thy wisdom; we glorify Thee for the wonders of the heavens and the earth; for the perfection of Thy counsels; for the riches of Thy mercy toward the children of men; for Thy saving grace and truth revealed to

the world in Jesus Christ; and for Thy presence vouchsafed to us through Thy Holy Spirit. All praise and adoration be given unto Thee, by day and night, with voice and heart, from generation to generation, O Father, Son, and Holy Spirit, God most blessed and most glorious, for ever and ever. Amen[11]

Then will follow the Confession of Sin, with the minister and the congregation joining in unison. In order to lead people effectively into the prayer, the minister may say, "Let us confess our sin before Almighty God. Let us pray"—

Most holy and merciful Father; We acknowledge and confess before Thee; Our sinful nature prone to evil and slothful in good; And all our shortcomings and offenses. Thou alone knowest how often we have sinned; In wandering from Thy ways; In wasting Thy gifts; In forgetting Thy love. But Thou, O Lord, have mercy upon us; Who are ashamed and sorry for all wherein we have displeased Thee. Teach us to hate our errors; Cleanse us from our secret faults; And forgive our sins; For the sake of Thy dear Son. And O most holy and loving Father; Help us, we beseech Thee; To live in Thy light and walk in Thy ways; According to the commandments of Jesus Christ our Lord. Amen.[12]

or

We confess, O God, that we have sinned against you, against ourselves, and against our neighbors. We have called on your name, but we have not done your will for us. We have esteemed ourselves, but we have not respected your image in us. We have sought the company of others, but not always their good. Forgive us, we pray, and make us what you desire us to be; through Jesus Christ our Lord. Amen.[13]

Some form of Assurance of Pardon comes appropriately here. Some ministers make this to be no more than another paragraph attached to the Prayer of Confession. It ought properly to be a declaration of the everlasting promise of God that whosoever comes to him in penitence and faith will receive pardon. As *The Directory for Worship* puts it, "Following the confession of sin, a declaration shall be made to the people of the assurance of their forgiveness in Christ. This should be done not as words which procure forgiveness, but as a declaration of all assembled of the reality of the divine mercy."[14] Such a declaration may be selected from the Bible:

> The Lord *is* merciful and gracious, slow to anger, and plenteous in mercy. He hath not dealt with us after our sins; nor rewarded us according to our iniquities. For as the heaven is high above the earth, *so* great is his mercy toward them that fear him. As far as the east is from the west, *so* far hath he removed our transgressions from us. (Ps. 103:8, 10–12, k.j.v.)

or

> If we say that we have no sin, we deceive ourselves, and the truth is not in us. If we confess our sins, he is faithful and just to forgive us *our* sins, and to cleanse us from all unrighteousness. (I John 1:8–9, k.j.v.)

The Prayer of Adoration should end with an Amen by the people. If the Confession of Sin is recited in unison there should be no Amen by either minister or congregation. The minister will then go right on into the Assurance of Pardon to which the people respond with an Amen.

The Preparation ends with the Hymn of Praise, "From all that dwell below the skies," by Isaac Watts, which is a brief, joyful burst of gratitude to God for the remission of the people's sin through the finished work of Christ.[15]

It may be noted here that the most appropriate way to call the people to prayer is by the simple expression "Let us pray." Never should a minister say, "Shall we pray?" or "May we pray?" as if the matter were being put to a vote or an appeal being made for a decision upon it; nor should it ever be embroidered with such pre-Copernican thinking as "Let us look to God in Prayer."

THE PROCLAMATION OF THE WORD

The Prayer for Illumination

With Calvin this prayer was usually rather lengthy and invariably very important. Its essence was the desire that the

Holy Spirit should so animate the read Word and control the preached Word that both might be received by the people in faith and obedience. Today, however, something more brief and simple is preferred. *The Worshipbook* suggests either the collect for the day or the following petition:

> Prepare our hearts, O Lord, to accept your Word. Silence in us any voice but your own, that hearing, we may also obey your will; through Jesus Christ our Lord.[16]

The Old Testament Lesson

It is customary in many Presbyterian churches to have Responsive Readings, generally from the book of Psalms. Opinions are divided over this practice. Critics say that it tends to neglect other parts of the Old Testament; that they are meaningless to most modern worshipers on account of the choppy character of a read antiphonal; or that they are a spurious way of engaging the people vocally in the service. An appropriate comment appears in a report of the Revision Committee on *The Book of Common Order* of the Presbyterian Church in Canada 1, 1956 (p. 5):

> It should be realized that reading a Psalm responsively cannot be regarded as a Lesson, for the Psalms are prayers and praises, not proclamation, as the habit of reading them responsively shows. Responsive Psalms serve the valuable purpose of giving the people a greater share in the prayers and praises, but they become spurious if made a pretext for omitting the Old Testament Lesson. . . . To read a New Testament Lesson responsively is another example of failure to understand what proclamation of the Word means. This is not the way to give people a greater share in the service.

Altogether it is better if ministers read an Old Testament Lesson meaningfully. Little would be lost if Responsive Readings were used only occasionally or not at all. On the other hand, in churches where the caliber of musical leadership is proficient, a Psalm properly chanted may follow significantly after the Assurance of Pardon.

The use of the Gloria Patri at the close of a Psalm is clearly explained by Dr. Coffin:

> In the second and third centuries, when controversies arose in the Church as to whether the God of the Old Testament is the God manifest in Christ, and whether his self-revelation as Father, Son, and Spirit is continuous with his self-unveiling to Israel, it became customary to affirm the identity of the God of the Old with the God of the New Covenant by concluding the chanting or reading of a psalm or psalms with the Gloria Patri. . . . This ancient canticle brings a selection from the Psalter to an appropriate climax. In view of the origin of the Gloria Patri, and its long historical association with the psalms, it is vandalism to tear it from its proper context and attach it to something else in the service.[17]

The New Testament Lesson

If this Lesson is properly the basis of the Sermon, or the scriptural presentation of its essence, then its selection must be made very carefully. In the above Service of Worship, since the theme of the Sermon is the Love of God, based upon 1 John 3:14–17, then the New Testament Lesson may be appropriately 1 Corinthians 13, Paul's great hymn on love. The value of the Lesson depends, however, upon its message and meaning being communicated by the reader with emphasis and effect. The following suggestions should prove to be helpful:

(1) The impact of the reading of Scripture is affected by the minister's own conception (of the nature of the written material). Is it read for the purpose of instruction only or primarily because it is the Word of God? Do these written words symbolize the concrete fact that once the Word became flesh? It makes a remarkable difference whether the minister believes the reading is merely from a textbook of moral maxims or the proclamation of God's redemptive note to his people in all ages.

(2) The minister should spend time upon the Lesson in order to master it. Effective interpretation depends upon

knowing the four *W*'s: *Who* wrote it? *What* did he write? To *whom* did he write it? *Why* did he write it originally? For this purpose he ought to keep within easy reach a compact one-volume Bible commentary.[18] (This applies only to preparation of the Lesson; the sermon demands much more.) Among the preacher's dictionaries and lexicons there should be included a handy reference guide to the exact pronunciation of biblical names and ecclesiastical terms.[19]

(3) Introduce the Lesson simply: "Hear the Word of God in the First Epistle of Paul to the Corinthians, Chapter 13." The conclusion should be equally brief: "Here ends the Lesson" or simply "Amen." An older form was "May God bless to us this reading from his holy Word, and to his great Name be glory and praise." Under no circumstances, however, should the message of the Word be embroidered with verbose flourishes or given the ridiculous appendix, "May God *add* his blessing to the reading of his holy Word." The Word is God's blessing; nothing needs to be *added* to it.

Incidentally, a liturgical aberration has been injected recently among our contemporary rubrics by the use of the unseemly form, "Listen for the Word of God." There is here, first of all, the implication that instantly we must sift out of the Lesson that which is the Word of God and that which is not. A rare competency indeed! Moreover, secondly, this rubric overlooks the difference between "listening" and "hearing," especially where the appropriation of God's Word is involved. Anyone can listen, but does everyone hear? The Old Testament prophets and lawgivers were sensitive to this human failing and hence they cried, "Hear, O heavens, and give ear, O earth" (Isa. 1:2); "Hear, O Israel: The LORD our God is one LORD" (Deut. 6:4); "Hear this word that the LORD hath spoken against you, O children of Israel" (Amos 3:1, K.J.V.). Karl Barth understood the difference in depth and effectiveness between hearing and listening when he wrote:

> "In the Church to act means *to hear*, i.e., to hear the Word of God, and through the Word of God revelation and faith. . . . in

the whole world there exists no more intense, strenuous or animated action than that which consists in *hearing* the Word of God."[20] (Author's emphasis.)

Hearing is our need because most people listen but do not hear. Only when they hear does the claim of God's Word get to them and lay hold actually upon their reason and will. Hearing, then, means "ceasing from every external activity and holding oneself still and prepared like a ploughed field in springtime ready for seed."[21]

(4) It is distracting to interject comments throughout the reading, especially if they refer only to the *minutiae* of language or word forms. It is helpful sometimes, however, at the outset to identify, for example, certain pronouns whose antecedents are named in a previous verse or chapter. In reading Luke, Chapter 7, the minister would begin, "After *he* [read "Jesus"] had ended all his sayings in the hearing of the people he entered into Capernaum."

(5) No reader should *recite* the Lesson. Such a practice calls attention to oneself, flaunts a sense of pride, and fills the listeners with apprehension lest one forget the lines. Moreover, no minister should present a mosaic of tidbits chosen here and there from the Scriptures. The thought pattern then is inherently his or her own and through clumsy eisegesis the reader tries to discover verses to put into it. It is not too much to say that this action outrages Holy Scripture.

Anthem

The Directory for Worship recognizes that no *rigid* pattern regarding the development of the service can be set. Moreover, since every minister must face up to the realities of the local situation and reckon with psychological as well as theological factors in worship, any decision relating to the placing of the anthem, for example, cannot be too arbitrary. Monotony in worship originates in doing any one thing too frequently or too long. This section of the service, the Proclamation of the Word, consisting of a minimum period of thirty to thirty-five minutes of reading and preaching, can droop unless there is at least one change of fare. Why not an anthem at this point? Also, no choir director who invests time and professional competence in the work and witness of a group of singers—call them auxiliary[22] or congregational—will be satisfied to present any of the great choral compositions of Christendom only "when the collection is being taken."

Sermon

Since this is not a book on the art or theory of preaching, it is enough to say that the nature of the Sermon must be "a responsible proclamation of the Biblical message spoken to contemporary life."[23] After the Sermon an invitation may be given to any persons "to renew their obedience to Christ or to make profession of faith and to unite with the Church."[24]

The Apostles' Creed

In response to the message of the Word through reading and preaching, the congregation will rise to repeat the Creed. Some persons feel that the constant recitation of a creed encourages the peril of familiarity and listlessness. Much depends, however, upon the manner in which it is said. The ministers should lead in the affirmations. Their stance will depend upon the interior construction and arrangement of the sanctuary. If there is a chancel, the minister may turn sideways with the choir in order not to be embarrassed by making the affirmations seemingly to the people's faces. Further, the minister should avoid the inclination to race meaninglessly through the Creed. It should be spoken according to the structure of its phrasing and with a measure of unaffected deliberation. There is much to be said for Donald Tytler's suggestion that the Creed be "introduced by the words 'We believe. . .' to emphasize that it is the faith of the community, not the faith of individuals, that is being affirmed."[25] (Author's emphasis.)

THE FELLOWSHIP OF PRAYER

The Offering

The service proceeds now into the second main movement: the offerings of the people are collected and presented. Every effort should be made by the minister and those who discharge this function to realize fully its meaning within the act of worship and to grasp its kinship to the larger program of Christian witness and service. Empty collection plates should not rest upon the communion table nor should they be placed there when full. Neither should the offerings be taken out by the deacons to be counted during the latter part of the act of worship. If the anthem is sung during the collection of the offerings (the advisability of this must be determined by the local situation), the deacons will come forward at its close and await a simple Prayer of Dedication by the minister. Care should be taken to vary this prayer weekly in order to avoid monotony. The full plates should then be placed on appropriately appointed credence stands or tables beside the Lord's Table.

The organist will play until the deacons (or ushers) have returned to their seats. It will contribute to the orderliness of the sanctuary and to the atmosphere or the Fellowship of Prayer if these persons will take their seats quickly and unobstrusively, and will refrain by all means from using this climactic period of the worship as an occasion for chatting in the narthex.

The minister leads the congregation in the great prayers of response: Thanksgiving and Intercession. Here any minister is claimed by a responsibility that taxes the acumen of one's personal devotion: as the spokesperson before God for the worshiping community, he or she must help the people "draw boldly unto the throne of grace, that they may receive mercy, and find grace to help in time of need."

The place and posture for these prayers will depend upon

the interior structure of the sanctuary. Ideally in the Calvinistic tradition they should be offered by the minister from behind the communion table and in a kneeling position. If, however, there is a large and elevated pulpit, with rather a diminutive table on the lower floor in front, then these prayers may have to be given from the pulpit.

Hymn and the Benediction

The final hymn may be a hymn of praise or thanksgiving, or a call to service. George Matheson's well-known hymn of dedication and surrender, "O Love that wilt not let me go," continues the theme of divine love and of how Christians are involved in it and encompassed by it as they go from the sanctuary into the world.

The minister will give the Benediction "in the words of Holy Scripture."[26] There is no rubric to indicate whether the congregation should stand or be seated with bowed heads. The Benediction, however, should be understood for what it is. It is not merely a formula of dismissal, the *Ite missa est* at the conclusion of the Mass; it is a blessing given by the minister, with raised hand, and it summarizes the whole service in the name of the Trinity. The solemn character of this act has been described suitably by George S. Stewart:

> When the minister comes to this last act in awe and wonder that God has commissioned him for this giving, the words will quiver and burn with the glory of their meaning—the grace of the Lord Jesus Christ—the love of God—the communion of the Holy Ghost—actually given as the supreme blessing to His worshipping people.[27]

II

Preaching in Worship

The mission of the preacher and the sermon in worship are inseparable. As *The Directory for Worship* says, "The preacher is called upon to relate the eternal gospel of the liv-

ing God set forth in Scripture to the life of the particular congregation."[28] This must be done, however, within the context
of an act of worship. How then does one describe the role of
preaching in worship?

A. Preaching must give content to worship. Since worship
is an expression of the faith of the congregation, then it must
be an *informed* faith. Calvin recognized early that the people's faith must be forever refreshed and strengthened by the
growth of knowledge, else it will be in danger of deteriorating
into emotionalism and superstition. "We ought not to attempt
anything in religion rashly or at random," he said, "because,
unless there be knowledge, it is not God that we worship, but
a phantom or idol." Real preaching presents a rehearsal of the
mighty acts of God which culminated in him who was the
highest redemptive event of all, and hearing it the congregation experiences a personal encounter with Christ. Preaching
tells them not only that God did something for us, but also
what and *how* and *why* it was done.[29] Preaching evokes faith,
but also it adds knowledge to faith. Preaching makes for an
informed faith. Worship marked by effective preaching will
call from the people a response not only with their heart and
soul, but also with all their mind.

B. Preaching must provide a living witness in worship.
Preaching can never be like a radio program that begins with
a flick of an electric switch. It is preceded by a written Word
that is read in the presence of a congregation, and then it becomes itself a witness to that Word through the person of the
preacher. Preaching is a living Word. It is, as J. G. Davies put
it, "an actualization of the Word which is read." And *The Directory for Worship* states, "... the preached Word, like the
written Word, points to the incarnate Word, and shows forth
the presence of Christ Jesus with power to save."[30] The sermon then is the preacher's own act of witness in which he or
she testifies to God's acts of love and grace and through
which God's "Thus saith the Lord" confronts humanity. This
becomes the most creative and prophetic act of all preachers.

It will involve and claim all their powers as scholars, pastors, and disciples, in order that their witness may evoke a true venture of faith on the part of the congregation. Moreover, the more fully they are grasped by the Word, the more likely will their preaching be seen and felt as a demonstration of the power of the Holy Spirit.

C. Preaching must be determinative in the act of worship. In a properly regulated service of worship, preaching provides a bridge between two acts, the reading of the Holy Scripture and the celebration at the Lord's Table. As Richard Davidson said, "The sermon is the proclamation of the message in the preacher's own words. It begins at the Scripture read; it ends at the Upper Room. If the sermon does not take the people there it has failed."[31] Preaching is never therefore an end in itself, nor is it done simply for its own sake. It is part of a corporate activity. A congregation of listening people is involved, and spiritually they are on the move. Reuel Howe has said, "The word spoken in monologue is a concluding word. The word spoken in dialogue is a beginning."[32] Every true sermon has a dialogical character. Its elements—declaration, probing, encounter, confrontation—are accompanied step by step by the willing assent of the people. This two-way action reaches its climax when the living witness and claim of the sermon bring the congregation to the offering of themselves to Christ as the family of God around his Table. Luther translates Romans 10:17, "So belief comes of preaching, and preaching by the Word of God." Through this preaching event Sunday after Sunday God provides for men and women the possibility of living by his grace.

D. Preaching in worship must be seen as an instrument of grace. This occurs in two ways: in an immediate, vertical sense as encounter; and in a horizontal developmental sequence as fulfillment.

True worship begins with God; he takes the initiative. Within the context of such worship, preaching channels to the people "the vertical inbreak of the Word of God."[33] For the soul that listens and receives, it is a gift of grace. Or as Paul

Tillich has said, "The Church is primarily a group of people who express a new reality by which they have been grasped."[34] This happens whenever the faith-filled preacher by whom the Word is preached confronts a community of people met with one accord in one place. In this unique fellowship, through the instrument of preaching, God's Word becomes a dynamic and redemptive factor reminding that through Christ one dies unto the old self and is re-created into the new.

Preaching is marked by this here-and-now complexion, but it has also an eschatological character that points to "one far-off divine event to which the whole creation moves." Along with Baptism and the Lord's Supper, preaching is a means of grace by which men and women are nourished spiritually unto life eternal. Through baptism people come into the fellowship of the family of God; through preaching their faith is articulated and given structure and substance; at the Lord's Table at each stated season their whole life is fed and renewed. Therefore preaching is in a sense the forerunner of the Supper. Without it, this sacrament would easily become a mere work of magic. On the other hand, as Jean-Jacques von Allmen put it, "without preaching the sacrament has nothing to prove."[35] Preaching that ends with itself is merely the discussion of an idea or the presentation of Christ as an acceptable model for moral character. But preaching that creates faith bears fruit finally in a union with Christ. "So we, though many, are one body in Christ," said Paul. This is the climax of the Christian's growth in grace. This is the fulfillment promised by the Word of preaching.

LITERATURE

Barkley, J.M. *The Worship of the Reformed Church.* Ecumenical Studies in Worship, No. 15. Richmond: John Knox Press, 1966.

Keir, T.A. *The Word in Worship.* London: Oxford University Press, 1962.

Paquier, R. *The Dynamics of Worship.* Translated D. Macleod, Philadelphia: Fortress Press, 1967.

MUSIC AND HYMNODY

Mitchell, R.H. *Ministry and Music.* Philadelphia: The Westminster Press, 1978.
Northcott, C. *Hymns in Christian Worship.* Ecumenical Studies in Worship, No. 13. Richmond: John Knox Press, 1964.
Routley, Erik. *Music Leadership in the Church.* Nashville: Abingdon Press, 1967.
———. *A Panorama of Christian Hymnody.* Collegeville, Minn.: The Liturgical Press, 1979.

3
The Sacraments: Baptism

In a paper, "The Sacramental Principle," submitted to the Church of South India, the following statement about the sacraments appears:

> ... the Sacraments of Baptism and the Supper of the Lord are means of grace through which God works in us, and that while the mercy of God to all mankind cannot be limited, there is in the teaching of Christ the plain command that men should follow his appointed way of salvation by a definite act of reception into the family of God and by continued acts of fellowship with him in that family, and that this teaching is made explicit in the two Sacraments which he has given us.[1]

The Directory for Worship of the United Presbyterian Church, U.S.A., says:

> In the sacraments, instituted by Christ himself for this purpose, the Church commemorates the redemptive acts by which we are united to Jesus Christ and made one in him. These sacraments, instituted in water, bread, and wine, are to be received in faith as the exhibiting and offering of the saving grace of Christ.[2]

Note particularly the following words or phrases: "means of grace," "God works in us," "plain command," "way of salvation," "family of God," "teaching is made explicit," "which he has given us," "united to Jesus Christ," and "received in faith." We are to understand by such terms in these statements that the sacraments were given to us by Christ and that under his authority and by his command they are to be celebrated and perpetuated. Moreover, since God's word and God's act are identical, the sacraments by their action proclaim and make presently real what God once did for us and our salvation. Hence they are gifts of his grace to the church through Christ for the redemption of humanity. Here we see dramatized God's re-creative and redemptive purposes on behalf of "fallen creatures in a fallen world"; and the assurance of forgiveness, of power, and of eternal life to all who receive by faith what he has given. They are the means chosen and ordained by him for declaring and bringing his love to us. The fulfillment of that act of love in us is union with Christ, and in this marvelous process, each sacrament operates according to its own intent. As Ronald S. Wallace puts it, "Baptism mainly bears witness to our initiation into this union, while the Lord's Supper is a sign of our continuation in this union."[3]

I

Meaning of Baptism

Baptism is one of the two sacraments recognized and celebrated by the Reformed churches. Incidentally there is only *one* Sacrament of Baptism; rightfully there is no such distinction as "infant baptism" and "adult baptism." *The Book of Common Worship* is entirely correct in drawing the distinction between the candidates rather than between the formularies, and thereby it avoids the misleading impression that there are two types of baptism. The chapter titles read: "The Administration of the Sacrament of Baptism to *Infants*" and "The Administration of the Sacrament of Baptism to *Adults*." The focus, therefore, is upon *the* Sacrament of Baptism, but its administration may be either to infants or to adults.

Presently, however, this is not our most urgent concern. What is disturbing, upon very little exploration of contemporary practices in the church, is to discover the extent to which for many people the Sacrament of Baptism has lost its original significance and basic validity. Indeed as a tradition it seems to be perpetuated by them for reasons certainly far less defensible than those which the early Christians felt were sufficiently authentic to initiate the rite.

In a discriminative article in *The United Church Observer*[4] entitled "Getting Little Nellie Done," Chaplain J. A. Davidson names two pressures that have done much harm to a proper understanding of the Sacrament of Baptism: superstition and social fashion. Once Emil Brunner indicated his sensitivity to the situation in saying,

> What does the fact of having been baptized mean for the large number of contemporary people who do not know and do not even care to know whether they have been baptized? Most of the contemporary neo-pagans have been baptized as infants. . . . The contemporary practice of Infant Baptism can hardly be regarded as anything short of scandalous.

Although this judgment may sound somewhat extreme, and his perspective may have been too European, yet he was uncomfortably right when he went on to call baptism "a highly questionable arrangement where it is requested more from a consideration of custom than from conviction of faith."[5]

Davidson goes on then to describe the reason for and the effect of this superstition with regard to baptism. He writes:

> The apprehensive parents fear that if little Nellie is not *done* something dreadful may happen to her. They tend to look upon baptism as something to be administered along with vaccination and the diphtheria and Salk shots—and generally they have about as much understanding of baptism as they have of the technicalities of vaccination.

Nevertheless, in view of this popular misconception one is not inclined readily to censure the parents as much as the church itself for its failure to take more seriously the religious instruction and care of its people.

The second pressure he names is social fashion, or within the framework of communal proprieties, "the thing to do." "This is the attitude of those," says Davidson, "who see the baptism of a child primarily as a social event" and hence a Christian institution becomes "a pagan birth festival" or "a bit of pious baby worship." This is accentuated especially when the parents express their preferences for having the baptism at home rather than in church. Then it can become merely a social conventionality attended by relatives, in-laws, and friends, and in all likelihood conviviality rather than Christianity is the primary order of the day.

There is, however, another misunderstanding: Baptism is regarded as something of an act of dedication. Certainly there is an element of dedication in every act of baptism, but there is much more involved than simply "a comely custom whereby parents may offer their child to God and seek the divine blessing upon his future upbringing."[6] Baptism can never be merely a dedicatory rite that overlooks the gift of God. However determinative and significant may be the thing that is done, its ultimate efficacy depends upon the primary fact that originally something was given. Baptism is the sign and seal of God's initiative taken in our behalf through his Son, Jesus Christ, and therefore the main thing is not what we do, but what God himself has done. Or, as P. T. Forsyth wrote, "Sacraments are modes of the Gospel (not of our experience). . . . Their standing witness is the priority of grace. . . . When we were without strength, Christ died for the ungodly."[7]

At this point it may be well to ask why these spurious interpretations of baptism have gained such currency among Christian people, even among those who are mature members within the fellowship of the church. The answer is simply that for many of these people the Sacrament of Baptism has never had any real meaning, and this chiefly because the teaching ministry of the pulpit has not taken careful pains to make it plain. They continue therefore to request baptism for themselves and for their children without adequate understanding of how responsibly they are involved, of the nature and reality of the benefits offered, or of the claims inherent in this work of the Holy Spirit. Few areas of the church's program and witness would appear therefore to be in greater need of clarification than the Sacrament of Baptism. Indeed the contemporary ministry, in view of this lack of parental understanding and of the rapid decay of Christian influence in the home, has a special responsibility in this matter and can restore the lost sense of meaning to baptism only by an interpretation that is biblically sound and theologically respectable.

A. Baptism is a decisive event in the life of every Christian. *The Directory for Worship* says, "It is a sign of entrance into the Church."[8] Or, as it has been put in *One Lord, One Baptism*, "The life of which baptism is the starting point is a life 'in Christ.' "[9] It is not the purpose of this essay, however, to trace fully the origins of the practices of Christian baptism, nor to enter the involved and time-worn arguments about the validity of baptism administered to infants versus what is commonly known as "believer's baptism." Large and scholarly monographs (see list at end of chapter) which have appeared from time to time have presented their respective cases in well-reasoned fashion, although most of them do little more than to help to solidify opinions and positions already held by opposing camps. In this area, cross-fertilization has been negligible. Yet few of us would cavil with George Hendry's point when he said,

> The withholding of baptism from infants would seem to imply that the gospel cannot be extended to us until we are actually capable of responding to it. But this is to impose a limitation upon God, which parents would refuse to accept in their own relation to their children; for they do not withhold their love for their children, or refrain from displaying it, until the children reach an age at which they can reciprocate.[10]

At any rate, whether one believes in administering baptism to both infants and adults or merely to the latter, there is common agreement that even before there were any church buildings and before the New Testament was written, the life of the church revolved around two focal points: Baptism and the Lord's Supper. Baptism was then, as it must be now, a decisive event, occurring once and for all, and as P.T. Forsyth described it, "It ended the way *to* Christ and began the life *in* Christ."

For those who administer baptism to both infants and

adults, the end and aim of the rite is, as Richard Davidson once said, "the making of a Christian man."[11] This, however, is a process; it does not come by fiat. In the progress of this person's spiritual development, baptism has a decisive place whether at the beginning or at the end. And the church is the context in which this process of growth and nurture, indeed of transformation, goes on. "Baptism is an act of the Church,"[12] and regardless of whether it be a little child or a mature adult who is baptized, it signifies the admission of another person into the fellowship of the church. "In all evangelical and Catholic Churches it is the act of initiation into membership in the Christian fellowship."[13] Or, to quote Davidson again:

> Baptism is the door by which all come in. The newcomer may be a man of years or an infant of days; the Church takes him up in baptism, and then fathers him, mothers him, brothers him till Christ is formed in him. Baptism is a step in the process of initiation into the family and household of God.[14]

Baptism of an infant differs in some essentials from that of an adult. The adult has come to an age of understanding and of his or her own free will consents to the enactment of this decisive event. But the child is different; the process is not complete until acting upon it at the eventual confirmation of these vows he or she unites formally as a member in full communion with the church. (Incidentally, it is quite improper to use the term "joining the church" in referring to the action of a person who had been baptized as a child. This person, by virtue of baptism, was already a member of the church, but at the time of confirmation responds to the church's call to acknowledge and testify to the work of God's grace in his or her life, and in the spirit of this profession comes now to the Lord's Table.) In both cases—child or adult—the purpose of baptism then is the same. "It initiated the baptized person into a new society—the Christian Church."[15] The difference with the child is that he or she must grow toward spiritual understanding and maturity, whereas the adult is able to appropriate these more readily.

B. Baptism is admittance into the Christian community.
With the increase of individualism in many departments of
the secular world, many people have lost sight correspond-
ingly of the communal nature and character of the church.
The idea of the Christian church as a community of believers
together with their children is a concept that should be more
clearly understood than it is today. Indeed this was the contention of Horace Bushnell in his *Christian Nurture* over a
century ago, in which he deplored the tendency of the evangelism of that day to overlook or bypass children and then
campaign vigorously to claim them in maturity.

> A pure, separate, individual man, living wholly within, and from
> himself, is a mere fiction. No such person ever existed, or ever
> can. I need not say that this view of an organic connection of
> character subsisting between parent and child, lays a basis of
> Christian education for nations, far different from those which
> now prevail, under the cover of a merely fictitious and mischie-
> vous individualism.[16]

Whatever may be said about the willingness of Jesus to
accept baptism from the hand of John, one thing is patently
clear: he identified himself in this act with the common life of
his own people. Certainly his experience at the Jordan was an
encounter with God in an awesome measure, but it was
within the context of fellowship and identification with a penitent people that the descent of the Spirit became intensely
real. Hitherto John and his followers were a little remnant
within the nation who were calling people to repent and turn
their faces to the kingdom. Baptism set its seal upon their decision to have done with sin and to embrace the new life.
Then the early church took over this rite and used it for admission to its fellowship. Indeed it was an easy matter to appropriate the practice as a symbol of cleansing from sin and
the acceptance of Christ as the Lord of life. And the sincerity
of their action would be endorsed by the gift of the Holy
Spirit (Acts 8:17; 19:6). This new life, moreover, was not
something to be experienced alone. It was *within* Christian
community. As Davidson has put it:

No one had this experience to himself. In turning to Christ a man became *ipso facto* one of the Christian company.... In the society of forgiven and forgiving men the new Christian learned more fully what it was to be forgiven; with those who were themselves wholly committed to Christ he discovered the dimensions of his new allegiance.[17]

Paul interpreted this act theologically in the early church as symbolizing our being buried with Christ in baptism (Rom. 6:4). The old life was submerged with Christ in his death and arose as new life with him through the power of his resurrection. But why the baptism of infants? J. Vernon Bartlett has made this observation:

The idea that a parent should enter a religion or covenant-religion with God as an individual merely, *i.e.*, by himself as distinct from his immediate family, would never occur to the ancients, least of all to a Jew. There were no "individuals" in our sharp modern sense of the term. All were seen as members of larger units, of which the family was the chief in the time of Christ.[18]

Whatever new departure the head of the household took, the family accompanied him. As John Dow wrote, "Just as a little proselyte was baptized into Judaism without his intelligent consent, so this feeling of solidarity would warrant the baptism of a Christian child."[19] Within the Christian family the child is under the influence of the Spirit of Christ from the outset because the family is in the community of Christ's church. This fellowship is marked by creative and purposeful activity in which God wills the good for the child as well as for every other member of the immediate family.

In view of the strategic and significant role of baptism in the growth of the individual into full appropriation of Christian faith and grace, ministers are duty-bound in this secular age to instruct parents and congregations in the ways in which their responsibility can be discharged fully and effectively. In the Reformed tradition adult baptism, on the other hand, presents no real problem. Once the sincerity of the candidate is ratified and an awareness of the redemptive efficacy of the gospel is demonstrated and confirmed, then the door is opened through baptism into the fuller use and influences of the riches of God's grace by the means he has appointed. When a little child, however, is brought by its parents, the intention is the same, but the timing and the involvement of the forces that make for ultimate realization are somewhat different. In the former, two parties are involved—God and the church; in the latter there are three—God, the child's parents, and the church of which they are a part—and each of these does something of real and significant consequence.

(1) *God does something.* Already we have seen that baptism is an event in which God, by his word, declares to the congregation—and in the case of the baptism of an infant, to the parents—his Fatherhood and the son and daughtership of his children. In the act of baptism the gospel of his saving grace is manifested and declared. As Hugh T. Kerr wrote, "In them [the sacraments] we *see* the Gospel even as we *hear* the Gospel through preaching."[20] (Author's emphasis.) And this act underscores the fact that God took the initiative in our salvation. Hence to point to the fact—or the argument, as in the case of the advocates of believer's baptism—that the infant cannot respond is fruitless, because God does not and need not wait. If and when the child grows up to be a redeemed person, the work of grace begun then and there in the act of baptism continues through the power of the Holy Spirit so that "[this individual] may increase from strength to strength and live in God's eternal kingdom."[21]

This is not to concur, however, with the Roman Catholic idea of *ex opere operato* which claims that baptism is an action having at its command the grace by which it acts and assuring the child of "baptismal regeneration." The fatal flaw in such a point of view is, as James Barr reminds us:

> to separate grace from the person of Christ, so that it becomes a kind of force . . . subject in some degree to ecclesiastical manipulation . . . grace is always the grace of our Lord Jesus Christ, and is in Him, and in Him only; grace is not something separate, which belongs to Christ, but is Christ Himself."[22]

Moreover the Baptist insistence that only through a faithful response can grace be received raises the awkward question: where can the Christian life make a start at all? How contrary this idea is to the testimony of the great spirits and saints of the Old and New Testaments and of the ensuing ages! Similar testimony was given from a Jeremiah who heard the word of the Lord, "Before I formed you in the womb I knew you, and before you were born I consecrated you"[23] to a Pascal to whom God said, "Thou wouldst not be seeking Me, if thou hadst not found Me."[24] Can we consider any child's life so common as to be immune to the claim of God's grace?

(2) *The parents do something.* By the questions asked and the promises made and sealed by prayer, the parents in the baptismal rite of their child enter upon a solemn and sacred obligation. It is the acceptance of a responsibility in behalf of another that is more absolute in its claim than the average parent is able or willing to imagine. Indeed the widespread flouting of this accountability to God and to their children is the cause of much of the Christian illiteracy of our day. For one of the main channels by which God's help can come to a child is the believing life and spiritual discipline of the parents. Indeed the extent of this obligation was spelled out early in the Hebrew religion and its implications have been carried over into the Christian faith:

> "Hear, O Israel: The LORD our God is one LORD; and you shall love the LORD your God with all your heart, and with all your soul, and with all your might. And these words which I command you this day shall be upon your heart; and you shall teach them diligently to your children, and shall talk of them when you sit in your house, and when you walk by the way, and when you lie down, and when you rise." (Deut. 6:4–7)

To disregard this command is to fail "to perform those things which God requireth of you, that the good will and pleasure of your heavenly Father may not be hidden from your child."[25]

This new transaction, moreover, was of the nature of a covenant. To God's pledge the parents respond with theirs in

keeping with the ancient terms of "stipulation" and "adstipu-
lation," denoting the declaration of the act of God and the response of the people, which, as we saw earlier, is at the heart
of all our worship. Every covenant, however, stands or falls
by virtue of the integrity of those who are bound up in it.
God's act is sure. From the parent's side, however, the indispensable ingredients are belief, faith, and hope. *Belief*: The
present directories for worship of both the United Presbyterian Church, U.S.A., and the Presbyterian Church, U.S., require that "at least one parent shall be asked to make
affirmation of faith in Jesus Christ as Lord and Savior" or "the
child to be baptized must be presented by one or both believing parents." Indeed, the United Church of Canada inserts in
the liturgy of baptism this arresting query, "Do you confess
Jesus Christ as Savior and Lord?" *Faith*: The believing parents, because of their own experience of salvation, declare
their faith in God's promises and they trust prayerfully that
given the right conditions, the benefits of his grace will be
the heritage of their child also. *Hope*: There is here, what
J. K. S. Reid has called "an expected faith." It is the hope of
believing parents that the child, coming to years of decision,
will ratify what is now being done for him or her by standing
forth as a Christian person. Together, in faith, they share an
expectation. And for this end and on this eventful occasion,
the parents pledge the resources and careful vigilance of their
life.

(3) *The church does something.* Baptism is a sacrament administered by the church and therefore it cannot have any
real meaning if it is separated from the the life and worship of
the church. Or, as Forsyth put it, "It is Christ doing something through the Church as his Body."[26] In baptism the
church in a sense claims the children for Christ and receives
them into its fellowship. For this reason the baptismal rite
should always be administered, except in very special cases,
"in the presence of the worshiping congregation,"[27] and so
also that the congregation in thus receiving these children
may promise with God's help to be their sponsors to the end

that eventually they may confess Christ as their Savior and Lord and come at the last to his eternal kingdom. In baptism the congregation rises therefore to a new level of responsibility, qualitatively and quantitatively, which includes and encompasses the character of its worship, sacraments, educational program, and even the physical provisions for the meaningful discharge of them. But chief among these influences is the spiritual essence of individual Christians who constitute the church's fellowship, for it is what Christians are that establishes ultimately the integrity of the faith we hold. Moreover, it is only this quality of life that can create and sustain that environment of faith in which the learning soul is assured of spiritual nurture. And who can estimate the results that can or may accrue when the life of one of God's children is constantly the focus of the intercessory prayers of that body of which Christ himself is King and Head?

One final word about the nature of baptism: in discussing baptism for infants and adults, W. F. Flemington said, "The one is starting a little farther back than the other, but both have a long way to go, and to each in baptism God offers himself with all the plenitude of his grace for the fulfilment of the purpose for which he created that human soul."[28] God is doing something here, and God is always on the move. The soul that has been brought by baptism into "the Spirit-possessed community of God's people" is nourished and built up by their contagious influence. There occurs then an unfolding of that person's inner life and worth and character, washed clean by holy love and saved daily from the powers of the world by the mysterious power of eternal grace, a process which can end only when each is fully identified with Christ.

ORDER OF SERVICE

Sentences:
Prayer (Thanksgiving for the church which provides this blessing; intercessions for the congregation and parents; petitions for the child; consecration of water to sacred use; petition that the action be to God's glory.)
Questions (Three in all, which may include assent to the Creed.)

Act of Baptism
Benediction
Declaration
Conclusion: The Lord's Prayer (In the case of an adult, the service
    follows the longer rite in the *Book of Common Worship*, pp.
    126–130. Candidate takes vows himself or herself and kneels to
    receive baptism.)

II

ADMINISTRATION OF BAPTISM

In order that the act of baptism be done with reverent propriety, the following suggestions are found to be helpful:

A. An attempt should be made by the minister to meet individually or in a group with all parents desiring baptism for
their children. In small congregations he or she has the advantage of being able to see each child in its own environment; in large suburban churches or in the case of a scattered
city congregation, a series of preparatory meetings at which
baptism is discussed and explained may be the more expedi-
ent way to handle the subject.

B. In a church with a large membership, certain Sundays
should be designated as baptismal dates and published
clearly in the weekly bulletin. In a small church this arrangement is not usually necessary.

C. The meaning of the Sacrament of Baptism should be
interpreted periodically in a sermon and should not be explained at great length during the actual rite itself.

D. Baptism should be administered at a point fairly early
in the service of worship. At the conclusion of the administration the parents should be advised to take the infants to the
proper nursery facilities, if available, and to return to the
sanctuary.

E. The minister should take precautions against mispro-
nouncing a name or, on the occasion of many baptisms, con-
fusing one with another. In order to assure individuality and a
more personal contact, each father may be given a small card

prior to the service, with the child's name inscribed upon it in bold type. At the appropriate moment he may hand this card inconspicuously to the minister, who is then able to proceed with facility and calm.

F. The Clerk of Session should assume responsibility in meeting with the families immediately before the service, regulating their entrance and withdrawal, and guiding them into their places, for example, at the chancel steps.

G. If the minister holds the infant, care should be taken to seat the infant upon the forearm, with the body supported by the holder's own upper arm and chest. Ordinarily it is a slight psychological shock to an infant to be transferred suddenly from the familiar arms of its parent to the strange grasp of the minister, and frequently the consequences are disastrous. At any rate, if the child has been received from one parent, the minister should return it to the other. Many ministers, however, consider it advisable to leave the child within the security of the parent's embrace.

H. The most meaningful and impressive services of baptism are done by ministers who know the rite from memory and thereby can create rapport with each family, which is impossible whenever one's eyes have to be fixed or riveted upon lines in a book. In both sacraments there is constant use of the hands; it makes for ease and effectiveness of movement if they are unencumbered and free.

I. It is unfortunate that the present *Book of Common Worship* so combines the questions into the lengthy statement that the point of each emphasis is rarely captured by the parents. The format, at least, in *The Worshipbook* is more simple, although curiously the Reformed concept of the covenant is omitted. *The Book of Common Order* of the Church of Scotland provides these questions:

1. Do you believe in Jesus Christ as your Savior and Lord?

2. Do you here present this child earnestly desiring that he [she] be received by holy baptism into the family of the Church of Christ?

3. Do you promise with God's help to bring him [her] up in the nurture and admonition of the Lord?

Perhaps the most recent, and indeed among the most meaningful questions are those of the rite of the Church of South India:[29]

1. Do you believe in one God, the Father, the Son, and the Holy Spirit?
2. Will you endeavor to provide a Christian home for this child and so to bring him [her] up in the worship and teaching of the Church that he [she] may come to know Christ his [her] Savior?
3. Will you endeavor so to order your own lives that you do not cause this little one to stumble?
4. Will you encourage him [her] later to become a full member of the Church; so that established in faith by the Holy Spirit he [she] may partake of the Lord's Supper, and go forth into the world to serve God faithfully in the fellowship of his Church?[30]

J. The minister should be aware of the crucial importance in the rite of baptism of the words "in the name of." The scriptural implications have always been *union with Christ*. In early Christian baptism it was a carry-over from the Old Testament idea that "the name of God was called over" and "put upon" Israel at the time of circumcision or the redemption of the firstborn (Deut. 28:10; Num. 6:22–27; Luke 2:21–22). But there are further meanings. It can indicate the source of the minister's authority; it is by the authority of Christ or the Holy Trinity that he or she administers baptism. Also, the phrase can be read *"into* the name of," which means "in the sphere where Christ works by the power of the Holy Spirit."[31] This latter meaning dispels any notion of baptism as being merely an act of dedication. In baptism we enter that environment of faith where God's acts in Christ are operative for our benefit and where we experience "a living union that grows throughout our whole life and is continually nourished by the Sacrament of the Lord's Supper."[32]

K. Occasionally a Presbyterian minister is confronted at a

baptism with an expanded retinue of attendants known as "godparents." Whatever may have been the origin of this custom or whatever may be their office in other denominations, in the Presbyterian tradition the godparents are the *congregation.*

L. On occasions when a large group is being received into full communion with the church, some of whom may be adults to be baptized, the minister should not make the service unduly tedious by going through each liturgy fully and separately. If it should be a case in which half of the group are to be baptized and all received into full communion, according to the *Book of Common Worship* (United Presbyterian, U.S.A.), pages 126 to middle of 129 may be used with baptizees, pages 131 to 132 with those united in full membership, and then pages 132 to 133 for the whole group.

M. In fewer areas of the complex life of a modern congregation does a minister encounter more baffling problems than in relation to baptism. Some of these contribute to a sense of perpetual frustration; others strain one's convictions and patience to the extreme. There will always be those cases—broken homes, mixed marriages, illegitimate offspring—in which only God's grace and an abundance of common sense will be sufficient. Each case, however, must be met and solved upon its own merits, and the minister's attitude must never fail to be *redemptive.* Each congregation, moreover, has its own customs and traditions, some of which may be merely the solidification of outworn, sentimental, and meaningless rituals, such as sprinkling the water by means of a rosebud. The directories for worship are clear in their rubrics: "The minister shall baptize the child with water alone." "[The minister] shall baptize the child with water, by pouring or sprinkling it on the head of the child, without adding any other ceremony." No one can effect a revolution in congregational habits in a day or a year, or maybe not even in the course of a whole pastorate, yet each enlightened minister must teach the people, beginning with the session, what in his or her mind and heart is felt to be right. Progress will be slow and be accompanied doubtlessly by many headaches and heartaches, but everyone who comes as a successor in the same parish will "rise up and call him [her] blessed."

LITERATURE

Arndt, E.J.F. *The Font and the Table.* Ecumenical Studies in Worship, No. 16. Richmond: John Knox Press, 1967.

Barkley, J.M. *The Worship of the Reformed Church.* Chapters IX & X, Ecumenical Studies in Worship, No. 15. Richmond: John Knox Press, 1966.

Barth, Karl. *The Teaching of the Church Regarding Baptism.* London: S.C.M. Press, 1948.

Cullmann, Oscar. *Baptism in the New Testament.* London: S.C.M. Press, 1961.

Jansen, John. *The Meaning of Baptism.* Philadelphia: The Westminster Press, 1958.

Lampe, G.W.H. *The Seal of the Spirit.* London: Longmans, Green & Co., 1951.

Leenhardt, F.J. *Le baptême chrétien: son origine sa signification.* Neuchâtel: Delachaux & Niestlé, 1946.

Marcel, Pierre. *The Biblical Doctrine of Infant Baptism.* London: James Clarke & Co., 1953.

Wainright, G. *Christian Initiation.* Ecumenical Studies in History, No. 10. Richmond: John Knox Press, 1969.

Warns, Johannes. *Baptism.* London: Paternoster Press, 1957.

LITURGIES (older authorized and modern)

The Book of Common Worship. The United Presbyterian Church, U.S.A., 1946 edition.

The Book of Common Order. The United Church of Canada, 1950 edition.

The Book of Common Order. The Church of Scotland, 1955 edition.

The Book of Common Worship. The Church of South India, 1963 edition.

Liturgie du Baptême. Communauté de Taizé lès Cluny (from the magazine *Verbum Caro,* No. 44).

4
The Sacraments:
The Lord's Supper

The Lord's Supper has been traditionally the central act of Christian worship. Here, as nowhere else, God gives himself to us through Christ. It is the supreme act of grace. However, "that grace is not a substance but the personal presence of Christ offering men a personal relationship."[1] We respond by offering ourselves to God in complete abandonment. In this encounter and its periodic repetition the human soul is nurtured and the integrity of God's promise is proved. This sacrament is the seal set by God upon that promise.

In view of the traditional significance and holy character of this sacrament, it comes to us as no little surprise that Walter Lüthi, the scholarly and well-known Swiss pastor, complained of "the plight of the Lord's Supper."[2] He indicated that in Europe today this sacrament "is rather generally in distress." Non-attendance is increasing because of what Lüthi called "the offense of the Lord's Supper." In America, however, this is plainly not a specific problem, although the predicament of this sacrament for other reasons is equally as real. Here the symptom, for example, is not poor attendance, which could provide at least a clue to or warning of an inner disease. More generally it is a false security produced by religious prosperity in which burgeoning statistics can render us insensible to real concern for the main thrust and meaning of this sacrament. As in the case of Baptism, responsibility rests primarily with the ministry, but at the same time a large measure of blame can be attached also to congregations whose members are apt to be frantically busy with religion while remaining quite indifferent to the essence and implications of its message and forms.

One of the more obvious concerns in the Reformed churches is what Raymond Abba calls "defective celebrations" of this sacrament. These occur through failure on the part of the people to acquire a thorough understanding of the sacraments and on the part of the ministry to recognize and grasp fully its own crucial responsibility in them. The sermon, for instance, in some services of Holy Communion is either omitted entirely or is at best a novel form of "meditation" intended to catch interest, but quite incapable of provoking even a lukewarm overture of faith. This malpractice arises not so much from an attempt to streamline the service of worship as from ignorance of one of the major principles of Reformed worship, namely, that the sacrament without the Word is empty. "In themselves and apart from the divine promise of grace," writes Wilhelm Niesel, "these signs mean nothing."[3] The water, bread, and wine are merely tokens and symbols of what is promised to us in the Word. And further, "the signs gather all their value from their vital connexion with the divine promise."[4] Or, as Calvin himself put it, "If the visible symbols are offered without the Word, they are not only powerless and dead, but even harmful jugglery."[5] And, "without the Word the Sacrament is but a dumb show; the Word must go before."[6]

Further, some celebrations of this sacrament suffer from the irresponsible or deliberate actions of some ministers who delete certain of its essential parts. In a sense, the Lord's Supper is a sacred drama and therefore whenever a scene is dropped or a major movement is telescoped for brevity's sake, the framework of the total action suffers from such wanton disruption. Who has not endured painfully the celebration of this service by a minister who, for lack either of understanding of our liturgical heritage or of a theology of worship, regards as dispensable the words of confession or consecration or *epiklesis*, and substitutes a truncated sacrament from which order, beauty, and meaning have fled?

This brings us to the frequently omitted factor: the character of the celebrant. Once Bishop Quayle, in one of his characteristic epigrams, said, "Preaching is not the writing of a sermon and delivering it; preaching is the making of a preacher and delivering *that*." In this process it is axiomatic that the quality of a person's moral nature is inextricably involved. By the same token, if the sacrament is the proclamation of the Word in another form, then is not this an occasion in which the inner character of the minister is under examination and judgment as probably nowhere else? There is a sense in which no one—not even the best among us—is sufficient to stand and officiate at the Lord's Table. It is unfortunate, therefore, that many theologians in their pains to establish the objectivity of the sacrament have emphasized its independence of the moral and spiritual character of the celebrant. In one sense J. S. Whale is quite right when he says, "The *validity* of the Sacrament is not destroyed because it has been celebrated by a man whose life is quite immoral or who has no faith at all. . . . The character of the ministrant is strictly irrelevant."[7] (Author's emphasis.) Certainly the power of God's grace cannot be curtailed nor its integrity undercut simply by the failures and foibles of our poor human nature. But, at the same time, we must realize that the objective validity of the sacrament and its ultimate efficacy are a continuum. Therefore one has only to ask the person in the pew, in whom the efficacy of the sacrament must come into its full circle, whether the response of faith is debilitated by the presence of a celebrant whose reputation is not blameless in the eyes of the community. I wager that anyone would be struck by the homely frankness of his or her answer. If a minister must earn the moral right to preach to people and if their acceptance of the Word that is declared is conditioned by whether that person lives his or her creed, by what strange law of impunity should the clergy's unrighteousness not interfere with the *completed* efficacy of the sacrament? And further, the sacrament, we noted, is effective through faith. This means that although the faith of the minister and congrega-

tion does not *create* the effect of the sacrament, it does imply
the essentiality of all partaking *worthily,* that is, "worthiness
. . . measured by . . . their grasp of what is extended to them in
the sacrament and of their own need of it."[8] Is it not a mutual
responsibility then of both minister and congregation in this
sacred enterprise so to prepare and qualify themselves spiritually as to make the benefits of this sacrament real in the
community to believers? To come with any other attitude is to
share in the guilt of Christ's death.

This leads us to the congregation. What numerous factors
contribute to the plight of the Lord's Supper among them! (1)
There is magic. Behind magic is the belief that if a certain act
is correctly performed it will produce certain consequences
automatically. It is an operation in which human technique is
everything and belief in a divine will is nonexistent. In view
of this, it is curious that some Christian people will deny ve-
hemently the Roman doctrine of transubstantiation and yet
continue to partake of the Holy Supper as a sort of talisman or
in an *ex opere operato* sense and have no hint of the place in
it of a responsible faith. (2) There is intellectualism. To others
the first main movement of the service of worship with the
reading and preaching of the Word is everything, and therefore the Sacrament of the Lord's Supper becomes for them an
option that is tacked on or an appendix for those who find this
sort of thing to be congenial. The author's first experience of
this kind of theological deviation occurred some years ago in
one of the Free churches in Britain. The morning service
ended and the choir and minister withdrew along with some
seventy per cent of the congregation; then after a recess, and
with only a fraction of the people returning, an abbreviated
and perfunctory celebration of the Lord's Supper followed.
What abiding significance or efficacious character does this
sacrament have if it is not treated as a vital part of the total act
of Christian worship? (3) There is the memorial. There are
more Zwinglians among Presbyterians today than one would
hazard to guess. True, there is a memorial element in any celebration of the sacrament, but the Zwinglian Communion

Service, to quote David H. Hislop, "adds nothing to the proclamation of the Word and is not in itself a means of grace," whereas Calvin's service was "a spiritual communion with the Risen Lord."[9] (4) There is isolation. The sacrament of the Lord's Supper is regarded and engaged in by many persons as an incident separate from the broad perspective of man's whole salvation. But as Wallace indicates, "Calvin looks on both sacraments as having the same end—to testify, and to assist in effecting our union with the body of Christ."[10] Or, as *The Directory for Worship* phrases it, "They [the congregation] participate in the continuing history of the people of God until Christ comes again."[11] Nathaniel Micklem outlined the broad dimensions of the sacrament in this way:

> There is first the backward look to the Last Supper and to Calvary—"in memory of Me"; there is, second, the forward look to "the bridal Supper of the Lamb" in the perfected Kingdom—"till He come"; there is, third, the feeding upon Christ by faith—"take, eat, this is My body"; there is, fourth, the Church as the Body of Christ—"as My Father hath sent Me, so I send you."[12]

I

In view of the shortcomings and misunderstandings described above, there appears to be an urgent need for a rediscovery of the meaning of the Lord's Supper in the many branches of the Reformed church today. Indeed, there is a desire for it. Donald Baillie therefore could not have shared Walter Lüthi's pessimism because he contended there was actually "a yearning for such a rediscovery and a feeling after it."[13] At the same time he was frightened by the fact "that we do not know exactly what we are doing, or why we are doing it, because we do not really possess a theology of the sacraments."[14] Maybe the best beginning can be made in this restoration of the meaning of the Lord's Supper by indicating its place in the worship of the church both as a seasonal recurrence and as a climactic event. *The Directory for Worship* says:

Since the sacrament is an action in which the whole Church participates and is part of the public witness of the Church to the power of the Word, it is normally to be celebrated as the culmination of the public worship of God, and shall not be isolated from the acts of worship which precede and follow it.[15]

And Raymond Abba wrote, "The Lord's Supper ... does not stand alone. It is the climax of Christian worship; a Sacrament of the Word, a sign and seal of the Gospel contained in Holy Scripture, declared in the Sermon, confessed in hymns and creed."[16] This is not to suggest that mere frequency of celebration will heal the current plight or alert the church to the dimensions of the present lack of theological and liturgical perception. It does require, however, that the sacrament be seen for what it is and that congregations come to it with a respectable and sober grasp of its meaning.

Already we have examined some misconceptions that are commonly held regarding the Lord's Supper. No one thinks, however, that these can be remedied merely by drama in slow motion. Competent teaching must be given from the pulpits of the church so that people will not feel they are called upon to observe two sacraments of the gospel instead of appropriating at a deeper level a gospel of the sacraments. As Hunter put it: "It is not in the Sacraments that confidence should be placed, but only in the God who gives grace through them. Grace comes with the Sacraments, not from them."[17] And this action of God is complete when the Word comes full circle in and through the believing congregation. The place of this sacrament then in our liturgical tradition will be meaningful and secure as long as church people see— as in the case of baptism also—how and why they are involved, the relevance of God's benefits to their common life, and the manner in which these come to them and are appropriated.

In the Lord's Supper, *something complete is given to the congregation*. Since worship is a two-way activity, it implies a reciprocal exchange between God and us. God speaks and we respond. In the reading and preaching of the Word God's nature is declared. But human words as the medium of ideas can be constrictive, especially since God's Word is infinitely more than lettered syllables and vocal sounds. God's Word is action. It is "his uttered will," to use Whale's phrase. And that will comes to its fullest expression in the life of his Son broken for the sin of humans. Therefore the Word is not completely declared until it is seen in this action. And the nearest to this action anyone can know on this earth is when God's giving of Christ for humanity is re-presented in the breaking of bread and the pouring of wine within the community of the children of faith. In this action, moreover, God does for us what we could never do for ourselves. Why did he do it? John wrote the simple answer, "For God *so* loved the world that he *gave* . . ." God is love, and grace is love in action. But grace is not something apart from God; it is his nature to love and that love is never static. It identifies itself with us in Christ so that by faith we may identify ourselves with him. And every time this action is seen at the Lord's Table, God seems to come nearer to us and we respond with a renewed overture of faith. Here is made present for humanity not merely the event of the Upper Room. Christians are living now on this side of Calvary and Easter Day. In the Holy Supper they see mediated to them and re-presented before them what God did for them once and for all on the cross. Here, in this sacred event, God's redemptive work becomes so real that they see what they are and they rejoice in the means he has provided to make them what they ought to be. Here, as J. R. P. Sclater said in *The Public Worship of God,* "is the Christian Gospel gathered into a sign." Here help is given as nowhere else. As *The Directory for Worship* states, ". . . in the sacrament of the Lord's Supper he offers [people] the continued spiritual nourishment upon which their eternal life depends, and he sustains them in the fellowship of the body of Christ."[18]

In the Lord's Supper, *something complete is offered by the congregation.* Much of modern worship is incomplete, disproportionate, and out of balance. But here in the Sacrament of the Lord's Supper, all emphases of Christian worship

are present: confession, thanksgiving, proclamation, consecration, and self-dedication. Moreover, it provides also the
means whereby the people in receiving the elements and "in
[their] response to the great gifts of God conveyed by them,
can show forth their faith in God by offering themselves to
him in love and praise."[19] But what is significant also is that
all our human faculties are involved as in no other religious
act. The people hear with their ears the Word declared; they
see with their eyes the action; they take into their hands the
elements; they taste with their mouths the bread and wine;
they assimilate into their bodies the symbols of a broken body
and shed blood; their memory plays upon the words "We do
this in remembrance . . ."; their imagination recalls the gar-
den, the cross, and the tomb; their conscience is examined as
they ask themselves, "Have we the right to be here?"; their
affections rise in eucharistic praise for what God has done;
and their will resolves to live in this faith "till he comes
again." And when they respond in this way, more fully than
in any act of worship they perform, to this complete demonstration of God's love, as Robert Bruce put it so well in the
first person, "We get Christ better than we did before." And
the greater the faith, "the better grip [we] get of Christ
Jesus."[20]

In the Lord's Supper, *something complete operates
through the congregation.* The Lord's Supper is a social act.
Basically each individual is responsible to come to it in faith,
saying in effect: "I must come, therefore, as Paul Tillich suggests, 'accepting the fact that I am accepted by God.' At the
same time I must acknowledge the tremendous truth that I
am here as a child of his grace. Only by the grace of God in
Christ am I here. But by virtue of the very nature of his grace
I am not alone. My brother (sister) is by my side. He (she) is
my concern and I am his (her) concern also. Both of us are
striving to fulfill the words of the great prayer the minister is
reciting, 'and here we offer and present unto Thee ourselves,
our souls and bodies, to be a reasonable, holy, and living sacrifice. . . . and we pray Thee to fulfill in us and in all people

the purpose of Thy redeeming grace. . . .' Here and now, if our faith is real, something happens through my brother (sister) and me: God's grace claims us one by one and makes us into his great family—the Church—around his Table." And anyone who does this acts as the Risen Lord who speaks to the needs of those who come believing.

Once Professor G. Johnstone Ross told of an incident that occurred years ago during the celebration of the Lord's Supper in a little mission church in New Zealand. A line of worshipers had just knelt at the altar rail when suddenly from among them a young native arose and returned to his pew. Some minutes later, however, he returned to his place at the rail. Afterward a friend inquired why he had done this, and he replied:

> When I went forward and knelt, I found myself side by side with a man who some years ago had slain my father and whom I had vowed to kill. I felt I could not partake with him, so I returned to my pew. But as I sat there, my mind went back to a picture of the Upper Room, with its table set, and I heard a voice saying, "By this shall all men know that ye are my disciples, if ye have love one to another." And then I saw a Cross with a man nailed upon it and the same voice saying, "Father, forgive them for they know not what they do." It was then I arose and returned to the altar rail.

Indeed how better could the communal character of this Supper be expressed than in these lines:

> Our presence there with others preaches a mighty sermon about Christ's promise. Together in this most solemn communion we declare that we are one with all other believers who have received and who are receiving the Sacrament; that we are one with all those who believe that the Lord who died for us is the One who is granting us his own body and blood, inviting us: "Take, eat; this is my body. . . . Drink ye all of it, for this is my blood of the new covenant" (Matt. 26:26–28).[21]

II

The shape of the worship prior to the celebration of the Lord's Supper is quite similar to the Ante-Communion liturgy discussed in Chapter 1, except for a somewhat fuller Approach.

The Call to Worship
The Hymn of Adoration
The Ten Commandments
The Kyrie: Lord, have mercy upon us.
      Christ, have mercy upon us.
      Lord, have mercy upon us.
The Prayer of Confession
The Assurance of Pardon
The Hymn of Praise (or Canticle)

Then will follow the Proclamation of the Word, including a Prayer for Illumination, the Lections, and the Sermon, and concluding with an ascription by the minister or the Nicene Creed by minister and people.

THE ACTION IN THE LORD'S SUPPER[22]

The sermon ended and the ascription given, the minister comes to the Table. After a slight pause and in an attitude of quiet devotion, he or she recites the sentences.

The Sentences

For God so loved the world ... (John 3:16).
For God sent not his Son into ... (John 3:17).
Greater love hath no man ... (John 15:13).
I beseech you therefore, brethren ... (Romans 12:1).

The Communion Hymn

During the singing of the hymn, two elders will remove the cloth from the Table and any other coverings from the elements.

An impressive Scottish tradition is the Great Entry with the procession of the elders bearing the elements. After the sentences the minister would announce the offering and retire with the elders to the vestry to be joined there with the deacons carrying the offerings of the people. Then to the accompaniment of, maybe Psalm 24:7–10, "Ye gates, lift up your heads on high" (Tune: St. George's, Edinburgh), the procession enters: elders bearing silver trays of bread, followed by others with the wine, and then the deacons with the collections. The minister, standing behind the table, receives the elements and the deacons deposit the offering plates nearby. (Cf. "The Holy Communion in the Presbyterian Churches," by David Cairns, in *The Holy Communion*, ed. by Hugh Martin, S.C.M. Press, 1947, p. 80.)

The Nicene Creed

If not already used, the people will rise and affirm their faith.

The Words of Institution   *1 Corinthians 11:23-26*

These words ought to be recited meaningfully and with due and proper care, for, as *The Westminster Confession of Faith* [U.P.U.S.A.] specifies [XXVII:3]: The efficacy of the Sacrament depends "upon the work of the Spirit, and the *word of institution,* which contains, together with a precept authorizing the use thereof, a promise of benefit to worthy receivers."

The Prayer of Consecration

Salutation: "The Lord be with . . ."
Sursum Corda: "Lift up your hearts . . ."
Exhortation: "Let us give thanks . . ."
Preface: "It is very meet, right, and . . ."
Sanctus: "Holy, holy, holy, Lord God . . ."
Thanksgiving: "All glory and . . ."
Commemoration (anamnesis): "Wherefore having in . . ."
Epiclesis: ". . . bless and sanctify these Thy gifts . . ."
Oblation: "And here we offer and present unto Thee ourselves . . ."

The Fraction and the Cup

Here the action should be reverently and impressively done. The minister will take a slice of bread (maybe 2 × 3 inches) and holding it in plain sight of the people, will break it, while saying:

According to the holy example of our Lord Jesus Christ and

in remembrance of him we do this, who in the same night in which he was betrayed took bread and when he had given thanks, as we do now give thanks unto Thee, O Eternal Father, he brake it and said, "Take, eat, this is my body broken for you, this do in remembrance of me."

The minister extends his or her arms as if to feed the group and with a broad gesture symbolizes the desire to include the whole company. Then he or she pours the wine from the flagon into a chalice.

After the same manner also he took the cup, when he had supped, saying, "This cup is the new covenant in my blood; this do ye as oft as ye drink it, in remembrance of me."

The minister lifts the cup while reciting and raises it to about midchest level, taking care to hold it without tilting and with both hands.

The Agnus Dei
"O Lamb of God, that takest away . . ."
(Sung in *lento tempo* by choir and congregation.)

The Pax
"The peace of the Lord Jesus Christ be with you."

The Distribution
The minister and people commune. The elders come forward and to each is given a plate of bread. As the minister gives the final plate to the last elder, he or she, recites:

The Body of the Lord Jesus Christ, which was given for you, preserve you unto everlasting life. Take and eat this in the remembrance that Christ died for you, and feed on him in your heart by faith with thanksgiving.

The minister is served by an elder. The elders themselves are served and then they bring the bread to the people. They return to the Table upon conclusion and resume their seats. The minister continues the same order with the wine.

The Blood of our Lord Jesus Christ, which was shed for you, preserve you unto everlasting life. Drink this in remembrance that Christ died for you, and be thankful.

The same procedure is followed as with the bread.

The Grace
"The grace of the Lord Jesus Christ be with you."

The Prayer of Thanksgiving
For all spiritual benefits
For the communion of saints
For faith to follow

The Lord's Prayer

The Hymn of Praise or Consecration
As the tune is being played, the elders re-cover the Table.

The Benediction
"The God of peace who brought again . . ."

III

In order that this service be most fittingly celebrated, the following suggestions may be helpful:

A. The Creed: The exact origin of the creeds is not clear, although we know that they were framed in earliest times by bishops and councils and were intended to be recited with the sacraments. The Nicene Creed dates from the Council of Nicaea, A.D. 325, and the Apostles' Creed reached its final form about A.D. 750. The Nicene Creed amplifies some of the clauses in the Apostles' Creed and therefore was preferred at communion and other great festivals for these fuller statements about the nature, life, and work of Christ.

B. The elements:

1. Bread: What was used at the Last Supper? If it were a Passover meal, unleavened bread would undoubtedly be used.[23] But this matter is still being debated and we have only the knowledge that in some of the earliest observances of the Lord's Supper the regular bread of the people was used. Then about the ninth century, because unleavened bread kept longer and because the Roman Church preferred that communion elements be different, its use became more

general. As early as the thirteenth century in England, wafers were made out of pure wheat flour and water, in the presence of a fully robed priest, and were stamped with the symbol IHS or AΩ. For the Roman Church these came into almost universal use and were called "host," from the Latin *hostia*, meaning "sacrifice." The practice in the Reformed churches, especially the Presbyterian, has been generally to use ordinary bread as being symbolic of that by which our common life is nourished and sustained.[23]

2. Wine: It is likely that red wine was used in the Upper Room, and for centuries the early church used it. Some diluted it with water, as St. Ambrose in the fourth century, to symbolize the blood and water that issued from Jesus' side on Calvary. Some others regarded the mixture as reminiscent of the two natures of Christ. However, with the spread of Christianity the celebration was performed in countries having little or no wine at all. In England, for example, the common drink was mead and since it was quite unsuitable for communion, the practice of "intinction" arose (from the Latin *intinctio*, meaning "to tinge"), dipping the wafer into the wine in the cup. This custom ran into strong opposition at first because for some the symbolism seemed contrary to the action at the Supper and because for others it reminded them of Judas' sop (John 13:26–27). In Europe the Roman Church in the Middle Ages circumvented the wine shortage by giving only the bread to the laity and requiring the priest to drink the wine in their behalf. Calvinists, however, have never been fully reconciled to the use of wine. In the United States prohibitionist movements opposed the use of wine in the late nineteenth and early twentieth centuries and therefore grape juice was used as a substitute. This custom has caught on gradually in the Old World and on the mission fields of the Far and Middle East.

C. Practical matters: The beauty and inspiration of the Lord's Supper are increased and deepened when all practical matters are carefully handled and clearly understood.

1. Everyone involved in this solemn service should aim at

order, efficiency, and reverence. This is not an occasion for an awkward impasse, haphazard movement, or unnecessary improprieties.

2. Elders should be informed plainly in advance of their every action and responsibility throughout the service.

3. The table should be prepared and set in order before early worshipers arrive. They should come into a sanctuary where all arrangements have been carefully executed in good time.

4. The communion vessels should be cleaned, polished, and cared for meticulously by a responsible person or committee. The Table of the Lord is no place for tarnished silver, crumpled linen, or any other evidence of indifference and disarray.

5. In the act of serving, the table ought to be uncovered with efficiency and skill. The uncovering of the table symbolizes the action of the early church when the worshipers brought in their gifts of bread and wine. The Eastern churches perpetuate this action in the Great Entrance, and a similar idea is suggested by the rubric in the liturgy of the Church of Scotland, "During the singing the elements of bread and wine shall be brought into the church and laid on the Holy Table." Also, since in Presbyterian churches the residue of the elements is not consumed by the celebrant and his or her assistants, nor are the vessels cleansed at this moment, then it would seem appropriate to cover the table after the concluding prayer and thereby connote the completed action.[24] There should be on the table a chalice of medium size for the lifting of the cup and an unbroken slice of bread for the fraction. Both minister and elders should handle plates and trays with the order and poise of those who deal in holy things, so that all may be at ease and in an attitude befitting the solemn occasion.

D. Increasingly there is a preference for silence during this service. As Hugh T. Kerr wrote, "It is a service of sacramental silence in which the voice of God is heard. . . . In these days when people are seldom alone, this period of si-

lence is a means of grace."[25] And Oswald Milligan remarked:

> Rightly used, the silence of a great congregation whilst commu-
> nicating may be one of the most uplifting and inspiring influ-
> ences that flow from the observance of the Sacrament. It has the
> inestimable advantage of providing a time when the voice of
> man being hushed, Christ is left free to speak his own word to
> the soul that waits upon him.[26]

Common experience has convinced us that the spiritual impact of this service is rarely deepened by sentimental organ
reveries or humming choirs.

E. Many thoughtful ministers deplore what is called
"simultaneous communion," the custom in some churches of
each member retaining the elements in his or her hands until
everyone is served and then all partaking together. Even at its
best this practice has little to recommend it. It is reminiscent
of a secular toast in a banquet hall. Indeed Dr. Kerr called it
"a reprehensive innovation." But all the more grievous, it is
an affront to the basic belief that our unity around the Lord's
Table is not a mechanical creation but issues from a deeper
source. It rests in our risen and living Lord in whom all children of faith are one.

F. Admission to the Lord's Table varies according to denominations and traditions. Extremes of laxity or exclusive-
ness do harm to the Christian fellowship. The United Church
of Canada, for example, borders upon widest latitude: "The
Sacraments of the United Church of Canada are open to all
who profess faith in Christ and God alone is the judge of that
faith."[27] Some other traditions, however, tend to be more
rigid and severe. Certainly the elements should not be given
to young children who have no notion of moral struggle or
have not made a pledge of discipleship, even if they were in
some ways spiritually responsible. This is the Lord's Table; it
is not the property of any individual person or congregation.
Those who are sincere in their desire to break with sin and
have pledged their allegiance to Christ in a public profession
of their faith should come; those who are satisfied to remain
as they are should stay away. As someone once put it, "The

Table is spread for sinners, but they must be sinners who wish to be made whole." No minister wishes arbitrarily to exclude any one soul in search of consolation, but each person's own conscience can know where the lines are drawn when the invitation to commune is put in this way:

> In the name of the Lord Jesus Christ, I invite to this Table all who are members in full communion with any branch of the church of Christ. The Table is his, and belongs by right to all his people. Any such persons present are lovingly urged to claim their rights in him.[28]

G. The question of private communions needs careful study because they are on the increase, especially with shut-ins, with the dying, and at weddings. A private communion is permitted by the United Presbyterian Church, U.S.A. and by the Presbyterian Church, U.S., although curiously enough it is forbidden in *The Westminster Confession of Faith* (XXIX:4). Such a celebration is regarded by the denomination as legitimate as long as an elder also is present to represent the church. Objection to celebrations at weddings is not against the act *per se*, but within the context of the Reformed tradition all present should partake. A private celebration for the principals at the chancel steps is alien to our basic presuppositions regarding this sacrament and even at best makes very little sense.

H. The quality of sacred music in most Reformed churches is improving both in performance and repertoire. No conscious attempt ought to be made to ensure better music on any one Sunday than another. Nevertheless special care should govern the music and hymn selections for the celebration of the sacrament. The Communion Hymn particularly should not be morbidly subjective but should point to Christ and his atoning work then and now. Some of the better hymns for this service are:

"Jesus, to Thy table led" (Baynes) St. Philip
" 'Twas on that night" (Morison) Rockingham
"Here, O my Lord, I see" (Bonar) St. Agnes

"According to Thy gracious word" (Montgomery) St. Flavian
"Jesus, Thou Joy of loving hearts" (Palmer) Maryton

The concluding hymn should sound either the note of praise or consecration:

"O thou my soul, bless God the Lord" (Psalter) St. Paul
"O Master, let me walk with Thee" (Gladden) Maryton
"Jesus, I live to Thee" (Harbaugh) Lake Enon
"O for a thousand tongues" (Wesley) Richmond
"All hail the power of Jesus' name" (Perronet) Miles' Lane
"Crown Him with many crowns" (Bridges) Diademata

I. It is unfortunate that services preparatory to communion have generally disappeared. In former years they held a significant place in the annual diet of worship in Presbyterian churches. Roman Catholics go to confession prior to Mass; Presbyterians used to prepare themselves for the celebration of the Lord's Supper, especially in the Scottish Highlands, with several weekday services. Local conditions affect the feasibility of such services today, but their usefulness, if rightly handled, commends their continuance. They provide a splendid teaching opportunity, a meaningful experience for new members, and an occasion in which the fellowship of the smaller group can be more intimate and helpful.

LITERATURE

Barclay, A. *The Protestant Doctrine of the Lord's Supper.* Glasgow: Jackson, Wylie & Co., 1927.

Burnet, G. B. *The Holy Communion in the Reformed Church of Scotland 1560–1960.* Edinburgh: Oliver & Boyd, 1960.

Clark, Neville. *An Approach to the Theology of the Sacraments.* Studies in Biblical Theology, No. 17. London: S.C.M. Press, 1956.

Cullmann, Oscar, and Leenhardt, F. J. *Essays on the Lord's Supper.* Ecumenical Studies in Worship. No. 1. Richmond: John Knox Press, 1958.

Davies, J. G. *The Spirit, the Church, and the Sacraments.* London: Faith Press, 1954.

Higgins, A. J. B. *The Lord's Supper in the New Testament.* Studies in Biblical Theology, No. 6. London: S.C.M. Press, 1952.

Lüthi, Walter, and Thurneysen, Eduard. *Preaching, Confession, The*

Lord's Supper. Richmond: John Knox Press, 1960.
Niesel, Wilhelm. *Reformed Symbolics*. Edinburgh: Oliver & Boyd, 1962.
Scott, C. A. *The Church, Its Worship and Sacraments*. London: S.C.M. Press, 1927.
Witherspoon, H. J. *Religious Values in the Sacraments*. Edinburgh: T. & T. Clark, 1928.

LITURGIES (older authorized and modern)

The Book of Common Worship. The Presbyterian Church in the U.S.A., pp. 155–175, 1956 edition.
The Book of Common Order. The Church of Scotland, pp. 111–148, 1955 edition.
The Book of Common Order. The United Church of Canada, pp. 75–96, 1932 edition.
The Book of Common Worship. The Church of South India, 1963 edition.
The Eucharistic Liturgy of Taizé. London: Faith Press, 1962.
The Worshipbook. Philadelphia: The Westminster Press, 1972.

5
The Wedding

Marriages, it has been said, are made in heaven, nevertheless they are not immune to various forms of earthly attrition. The Census Bureau and the National Center for Health Statistics report that in 1978 there were 1.1 million divorces in the United States—and 2.2 million marriages—making the divorce rate 5.1 per 1,000; moreover, the number of unmarried couples living together has more than doubled since 1970.[1] This situation presents modern ministers with a problem of serious dimensions because it strikes a crippling blow against the basic unit of church and society, namely, the Christian home. At the same time it beats against them personally and professionally because the many hours spent in remedial counseling constitute one of the most wearying aspects of the pastoral ministry. It is not surprising, therefore, that a grave concern for the welfare of the marriage institution is shared by the clergy of all denominations. Indeed it can be said—and fortunately so—that many Protestant ministers have acquired more competence and skill in marriage counseling and instruction than in any other area of congregational responsibility.

Every minister knows that in performing a marriage he or she is responsible to both the state and the church. Since marriage is a civil contract it comes under the jurisdiction of the laws of the state. Indeed the state can, and usually does, provide through its magistrates the means for fully legal marriages outside the sanction of the church and irrespective of religious organizations. A minister, however, cannot perform a marriage ceremony in the church unless the parties involved have complied with the legal requirements of the state. On the other hand, even after the civic law has been satisfied, conscientious ministers will not lose sight of the fact that they represent the church, and for this reason occasionally may refuse on moral considerations to marry two persons to whom the state had given through a license its prior consent.[2] The consent of the state denotes merely that the man and woman have now the right to live together without criticism from society or punishment by law, but ministers must be convinced within themselves that the union has also the approval of God. The involvement of the church, therefore, deepens the seriousness of the matter and points the minister to a third and very exacting responsibility: the personal. The laws of the state and the sanctions of the church are set down in specific rules, but the personal must take into account the preparation for the marriage, the meaning of the new partnership, the significance of the service in which the ceremony takes place, and maybe later the salvaging of that one union in four that is about to dissolve.

Although many customs related to marriage, particularly the actual ceremony, have changed considerably through the centuries, Christianity has taken pains increasingly to claim for it a dimension that earlier forms and practices did not suggest or imply. This dimension is implied in the vocabulary used in the Christian wedding service: "The solemnization of marriage"; "the holy estate of matrimony"; "blessed by our Lord Jesus Christ and to be held in honor among all people." These indicate the church's hallowing of what was once an institution of the natural order taking place in a purely domestic situation and with a ceremony of Greco-Roman character. Protestantism, however, has never gone so far as to institute a sacrament of marriage. Indeed it was not until the fourth century that marriage was regarded as a Christian sacrament, and even then it was merely a matter of attaching the Eucharist to rites that were pagan anyway.[3]

In keeping with the church's effort and concern, *The Directory for Worship* calls its chapter significantly, "The *Sanctifying* of Marriage." Here two emphases are singled out: (1) instruction in the meaning of Christian marriage; and (2) the wedding ceremony as a service of worship before God. The latter is our chief interest by reason of the subject matter of this volume, yet there are a few general observations that can be made about the first that are outside of the more technical provinces of psychology, sociology, and pastoral care.

(1) *The meaning of marriage:* "A true marriage," wrote Frederick W. Brink, "is the blending of the personalities of one man and one woman into each other for the advancement of both together."[4] This relationship is not held by physical attraction alone, but through a bond of mutual love that issues in the pursuit of common interests and goals: a Christian home, a respectful family, and the fulfillment of two personalities through each other and with God's help. Ideally life must always be a human response to God's acts of love and grace. In married life a man and woman discover in their partnership that this response is more meaningful than it was as single individuals. Moreover, within the community of the Christian home it initiates a new and stronger creativity and its by-products are of the essence of happiness.

Preparation for marriage includes a series of counseling sessions on the physical, mental, and moral aspects of the wedded life, but a careful grasp and understanding of what the service itself specifies should not be overlooked. The liturgy ought to be read phrase by phrase by the couple individually and together, and every term clearly explained by the minister. What is meant by "any impediment"? "In the covenant of their God"? "Pledge thy troth"? But chiefly it should be impressed upon every couple that there is a higher dimension suggested here:

> Marriage is not a simple contract; it is a solemn vow before God. Even if it is not a sacrament, it is sacramental. . . . Marriage is more than a physical union, however permanent; more than a mating of minds. It is a meeting of souls, souls which although eternally separate, can grow into a harmony such as no other human relationship can make possible. . . . Marriage affects personality for good or ill, more deeply than anything else in human life.[5]

Through marriage then the couple enters voluntarily into a new status. It is created by themselves. The church merely blesses and makes explicit what is implicit already in their consent. "They marry themselves," wrote F.W. Brink, "in the presence of God."[6] But with God thus in it, the potential for personal development and spiritual growth is boundless. What is more, it has a sacred character. And like every covenant made with God as a contributing partner, it is permanent. The contracting parties exchange vows which conclude with the words "as long as we both shall live."

(2) *The wedding service:* One of the many valuable results of the contemporary interest in meaningful worship has been an eagerness to reclaim the wedding ceremony as a Christian service. This does not imply that hitherto the service had been pagan; its liturgy is definitely Christian. But what was happening clearly indicated that social customs and secular pressures were claiming excessive recognition and therefore the congregations at many weddings appeared to attend for interests other than those normally entertained in a service of Christian worship. Further, with the increase of civil ceremonies, which may be after all a fortunate provision for unbelievers, the minister must make clear to persons contemplating marriage what the basic differences are. The civil ceremony establishes a bond by law; unlike the religious ceremony it takes no cognizance of why this marriage has occurred or what must be done in order to develop its meaning and to safeguard its future. The chief difference, however, is that it lacks "the self-giving of two persons to God in their new oneness with each other."[7]

(a) *The rehearsal:* The first step in making the wedding service a meaningful act of worship for all must be taken at the rehearsal. The minister who directs the proceedings will save him or herself unnecessary trouble if the matter of options is kept at a minimum. Indeed one may have to be firm in a kind way and assert, "This is how we do it." Some of these matters are settled earlier during the counseling sessions, especially regarding the folly of elaborate displays and lavish expenditures. Any couple can be advised quietly and in such a way that their sense of values becomes readjusted and a choice of dignified simplicity is made to appear more congruous with Christian worship.

It is preferable to hold the rehearsal one or two days prior to the wedding date and to have all persons involved in the ceremony attend, including if possible the parents of both parties. When all have assembled, the minister should invite them to sit in the front pews and by attitude and decorem give every indication that the importance of the proceedings demands that there be no hurry. A short prayer may be offered and then in a few well-chosen words the rehearsal can be lifted above the level of fancy and frivolity to reverent preparation. In this way, writes Joseph McCabe, "the rehearsal time will be redeemed for a spiritual purpose."[8] Then all involved are asked to take the actual places they will hold during the wedding service. The role of each is explained and demonstrated. Now they are told to disperse to the places they will occupy when the service begins, and then without music each moves as directed to his or her appointed location. This latter action is repeated, this time with music. When all appears to be satisfactory the minister will suggest that the wedding party, except the principals, retire and at the chancel steps (or at the appropriate place) a careful rehearsal is done of the major sections of the service, according to *The Book of Common Worship* or *The Worshipbook.*

(b) *The service:* On the day of the wedding all arrangements in the sanctuary—flowers, candles, and pew reservations—should be completed an hour before the appointed time for the service. The ushers ought to arrive early in order to check every detail, as well as to receive a quick preliminary briefing regarding their individual responsibilities. Each usher asks guests as they arrive whether they are friends of the bride or groom, and offering a woman his right arm (incidentally, there is no reason why all the ushers should be male), with the husband or escort following, will conduct them to their seats. The groom and best man meet in the vestry with the minister. The father and mother of the groom are ushered in just before the bride's mother. Two ushers come forward and unroll the white aisle covering, and when they have reached the back of the sanctuary the signal is given to the organist to begin. The minister enters, followed by the groom and best man, who take their places at his left. The bride's mother rises and the congregation follows (see diagram No. 1).

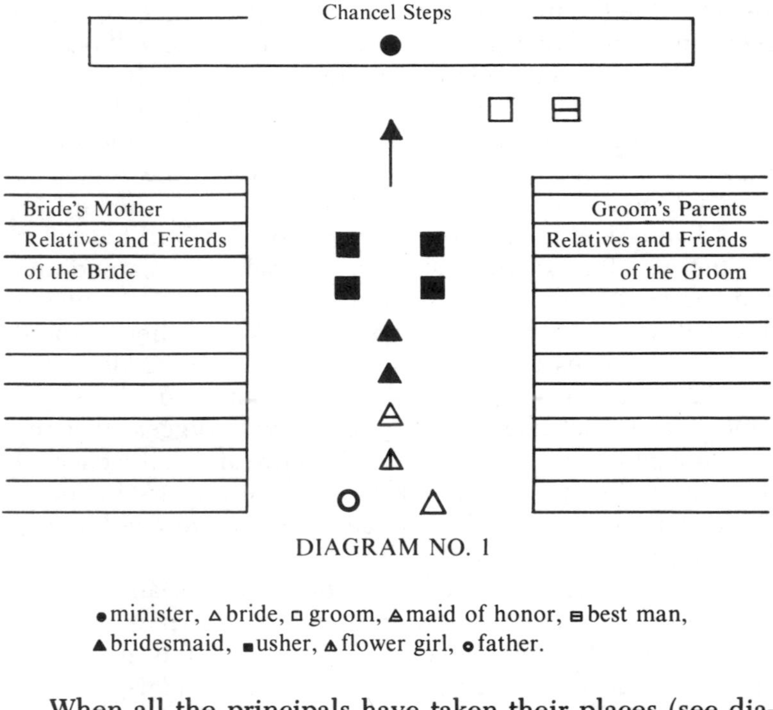

DIAGRAM NO. 1

● minister, △ bride, □ groom, ▲ maid of honor, ▤ best man,
▲ bridesmaid, ▪ usher, ▲ flower girl, ○ father.

When all the principals have taken their places (see diagram No. 2), the minister will begin by reading the preliminary statement about the nature of Christian marriage. This is addressed in an audible voice to the whole company. Then follows the charge that is directed to the bride and groom only. A prayer is offered and the questions of intention are asked. The bride is given away by her father who answers "I

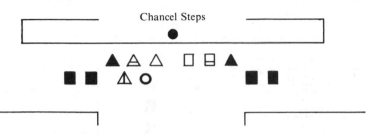

DIAGRAM NO. 2

●minister, △ bride, ◻ groom, ▲maid of honor, ▣ best man,
▲bridesmaid, ■usher, ▲ flower girl, ○father.

do" and places her right hand in the hand of the minister who
in turn joins it with the right hand of the groom for the exchange of the vows. At this point the father retires to the first
pew with the bride's mother; the maid of honor lifts the
bride's veil and receives her flowers.

Some brides prefer to be given away by both parents and
in such instances the father would respond, "Her mother and
I do." This form suggests the more preferable notion that by
their presence and witness the parents are taking notice "for
all the family of the passage of the daughter to her own household."[9] Moreover, it blunts the ancient image of women as
"chattels" which is suggested by the traditional question to
the father, "Who gives the woman to be married to this man?"
Indeed a much more appropriate form is recommended by
Khoren Arisian as follows: "Will you, their parents, grant
them your blessings and pledge them your love and acceptance?" To which they answer, "We will."[10]

The couple, with the best man and maid of honor, may
now proceed into the chancel where either a *prie-dieu* or a
kneeling cushion has been placed. The vows are performed
and the ring ceremony is completed. The newlywed persons
kneel for the prayer and the Lord's Prayer. When they rise the
declaration of the marriage is read, the benediction is pro-

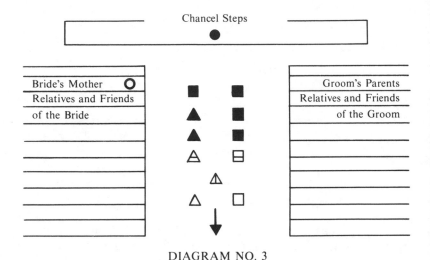

DIAGRAM NO. 3

●minister, △ bride, ▫groom, ▲maid of honor, ⊟best man,
▲bridesmaid, ▪usher, ▲flower girl, ○father.

nounced, and the recessional music begins. The wedding
party leaves in the order suggested in diagram No. 3.

In recent years, efforts by ministers to make the wedding
service more complete and meaningful have emphasized not
only reverence and decorum, but also the choice of appropriate music and the addition of elements traditionally used in
the regular Sunday worship of the congregation. The customary music, both vocal and instrumental, which has had purely
secular origins and associations, is being ruled out gradually
and some of the great hymns and compositions of our Christian heritage are being adopted. Young couples may ask for
popular folk/rock songs, show music, or movie theme music.
This, too, should be strongly discouraged. A good compro-
mise is to suggest that this type of music be saved for the reception. The minister needs to be supportive of the musician
in his or her stand and it may be wise to have the church

adopt a policy against such secular music. Old favorites of secular vintage, such as the solos "Because," "I love you truly," "Where'er you walk," and the marches of Wagner and Mendelssohn were never intended for use in a religious ceremony. The "Bridal Chorus" from Wagner's *Lohengrin* suffers from its association with the silly parody "Here comes the bride," but its fitness in a Christian service is questionable particularly in view of its origin. It occurs in the opera *after* the wedding in an atmosphere of distrust and hatred that ended in death and separation. Equally unsuitable is Mendelssohn's recessional march from *Incidental Music* which he wrote for Shakespeare's *A Midsummer Night's Dream*. This is played before Act IV in which Bottom, the weaver, is transformed into an ass, with all the later clowning and hilarity he produced.

A discerning organist will suggest processional music expressing a mood of dignity and joy, such as John Stanley's "Voluntary in D" from *Ten Voluntaries, Opus 6;* Jeremiah Clarke's "Trumpet Voluntary" (falsely attributed to Purcell); or Johannes Brahms' "St. Anthony Chorale" from *Variations on a Theme by Haydn.* Suitable hymns are: "Praise, My Soul, the King of Heaven"; "Praise Ye the Lord, the Almighty"; "The King of Love My Shepherd Is"; "Sing Praise to God Who Reigns Above"; "Joyful, Joyful We Adore Thee" or "Be Thou My Vision." Suggested recessionals are Purcell's "Trumpet Tune in D"; Campra's "Rigaudon"; or Marcello's "Psalm 19: The Heavens Are Telling." For pre-service music most airs and preludes from Baroque collections would be appropriate as well as: Bach's or Brahms' "Deck Thyself, My Soul, with Gladness"; Pachelbel's "Kanon"; Bach's "Arioso" from *Klavier Concerto in F Minor;* Bach's "Air on the G String" from *Suite in D;* or Vaughan Williams' "Rhosymedre." The selection of music of strictly religious character will occur more generally when all weddings are regarded as services of worship. Such music will not be judged by the standards of entertainment, but by its worthiness to be offered to the glory of God.

The following is a suggested order for a wedding service that denotes the church at worship:

Organ Prelude: Handel, "Aria" from *Tenth Organ Concerto*
               Bach, "Jesu, Joy of Man's Desiring"
               Sowerby, "Carillon"
Call to Worship
Processional Hymn "Love divine, all loves excelling" Hyfrydol
Charge to Congregation   *The Book of Common Worship,* p. 183
Prayer of Confession
Assurance of Pardon
Scripture   Ephesians 5:22–33
Charge to the Couple (a brief homily)
Questions of Intent
Giving of the Bride
The Marriage
               Declaration of Vows
               Exchange of Rings
Prayers and Lord's Prayer
Declaration of Marriage
Benediction
Recessional: Purcell, "Trumpet Tune in D"

For this service a regular bulletin would be provided for each worshiper.[11] The cover should be embossed tastefully with a Christian symbol and on the back would appear a statement concerning the meaning of Christian marriage and a brief prayer for those about to enter the wedded life. Inside, the service and marriage liturgy would appear in full, including the words of the hymn, the prayer of confession, and any other parts which the congregation may be invited to share.

Many ministers, in consultation with their sessions, have prepared a pamphlet containing useful suggestions to guide persons contemplating marriage. The following recommendations will be helpful:

(1) The minister should be advised by the bride as early as possible of the date of the wedding in order that all necessary arrangements may be handled conveniently and without pressure. Such advance planning includes the organist also. Consultation appointments and selection of music may be

made as late as one month prior to the wedding, but more time should be allowed if hymns, soloist, or extra instrumentalists are to be included.

(2) No minister is satisfied to have a wedding date precipitated suddenly, unless in unusual circumstances, and therefore he or she will not fail to require a series of interviews when counsel will be given to the couple on the nature, ideals, and responsibilities of marriage. (In some large churches schools of instruction for prospective brides and grooms are held at stated intervals as part of the adult education program.)

(3) Since the worship in Presbyterian churches is under the control of the minister and the session, the bride should indicate clearly her plans for the wedding service and agree that, within a certain reasonable latitude, the music, decorations, and other matters of conduct be subject to their approval and review.

(4) Photographers shall refrain from taking pictures during the wedding service and all well-wishers should be prevented from throwing confetti and rice within the narthex of the church.

(5) The couple may wish to have another minister (a brother, sister, classmate, or close friend) officiate at the ceremony. This is permissible, but the arrangements should be made through the minister of the congregation, who ought to be invited to have a part in the ceremony (unless he or she declines) and be consulted on matters pertaining to the use and traditions of his or her own church. The bride should not ask her minister to conduct the wedding service in a local church other than the minister's own, except in the case of a college chapel.

(6) The minister does not set a fee for the performance of the wedding service. The professional services of others are involved, however. The session, in consultation with the trustees, should have in writing and make available to the church staff a scale of fees for the use of the church building (if the principals are not members), for the organist, sexton,

and housekeeper (in this latter case, only if the reception is held in the parish house).

(7) The minister's formal responsibility ends at the church. If, however, the couple wish that the minister and spouse attend the reception, they should invite them in advance and, if it is a formal dinner with a toast to the bride, should plan carefully each conventional sequence. Nothing mars or makes anti-climactic the social sequel to a Christian wedding service more than a series of toasts by inept persons who, in striving to be funny, end up by being foolish.

(8) Every couple should take care not to be insensitive in the church or its immediate environment to the opinions and convictions of the minister and other persons regarding tobacco and alcoholic beverages. Some people thoughtlessly create offense which with the proper precaution they would not do willfully.

(9) When the newly married couple establish themselves in their first home, they should be encouraged to identify themselves early with some church and thereby claim by their action the blessings their wedding service presumed and pledged.

LITERATURE

1. On Marriage:

Brink, Frederick W. *This Man and This Woman*. New York: Association Press, 1948.

Easton, B.S., and Robbins, H.C. *The Bond of Honour*. New York: The Macmillan Co., 1938.

Mace, David. *Whom God Hath Joined*. Philadelphia: The Westminster Press, 1954.

Pike, James. *If You Marry Outside Your Faith*. New York: Harper and Brothers, 1954.

Sweazey, George E. *In Holy Marriage*. New York: Harper and Row, Publishers, 1966.

2. The Wedding:

Arisian, Khoren. *The New Wedding: Creating Your Own Marriage Ceremony*. New York: Random House, 1973.

Kirschenbaum, Howard & Stensrud, Rockwell. *The Wedding Book:*

Alternative Ways to Celebrate Marriage. New York: Seabury Press, 1974.

PAMPHLET

Responsible Marriage and Parenthood. The United Presbyterian Church (adopted by 174th General Assembly, 1962).

LITURGIES (older authorized and modern)

The Book of Common Worship. The United Presbyterian Church, pp. 183–192, 1946 edition.

The Book of Common Worship. The Church of South India, pp. 139–147, 1963 edition.

The Worshipbook. The United Presbyterian Church, pp. 65–68, 1972 edition.

The Book of Common Order. The Presbyterian Church in Canada, 1964 edition.

McCabe, Joseph. "The Marriage Service." *Service Book for Ministers.* New York: McGraw-Hill Book Co., 1961.

MUSIC

Wedding Music. Parts I and II. St. Louis: Concordia Press, 1952.

Music for Church Weddings. Greenwich: Seabury Press, 1952.

A First and Second Book of Wedding Pieces. London: Oxford University Press, 1960.

Baroque Music for Manuals II. St. Louis: Concordia Publishing House, 1977.

6
The Funeral

Arthur Reynolds in an essay, "The Shepherd of Souls," makes this timely comment, "It is a pity and a shame that in two matters—weddings and funerals—the Reformed Churches have so far lost control that as ministers we find ourselves officiating at what are often rather pagan ceremonies."[1] A liturgical authority, Von Ogden Vogt, once defined more specifically what Dr. Reynolds doubtless had in mind, at least concerning the funeral:

> The typical objections to prevalent customs are many: the excessive floral display, the elaborate coffin with its quilted satin lining, the super-refinements of the mortician's art, the morbid curiosity, the unseemly play upon the emotions, the undertakers' announcements, the procession to "view the remains," the sentimental hymns and syrupy music, the unwarranted costs, the easy assurances of faith that cannot be so cheaply held and, contrariwise, the lack of noble expression for vigorous conceptions of life and death.[2]

Among the more promising signs in the past decade has been the appearance of wise and dedicated ministers who have passed censure upon these customs and in their own parishes have taken positive and determined action to make funerals more definitely Christian. With characteristic frankness Roy A. Burkhart once said that at the beginning of his ministry he looked upon the funeral as something that had to be endured. Later he saw it as "an unusual opportunity."[3] And more recently Joseph E. McCabe has written, "Most funeral services bear little relation to that sense of victory which throbs on every page of the New Testament since Christ rose from the dead."[4]

In any attempt to improve the common attitude to funerals, it would be ridiculous to begin by laying the blame for every indiscretion upon any one person or group exclusively. Indeed it is only honest to attribute these faults to ministers, families, and funeral directors alike, because in most of the lamentable situations all three groups bear some share of responsibility. Either consciously or unconsciously they have held on to practices, points of view, and traditions that have no longer any place in the modern world and certainly ought never to have been countenanced in Christian communities. However, just as in every other attempt to restore the Christian emphasis to those rites of the church that have become paganized, the minister must initiate some careful strategy and by tactful methods and means make the people see their responsibilities as true believers.

One of the most effective ways is through a teaching ministry from the pulpit. Congregations are eager to know what the New Testament has to say about such common yet puzzling issues as grief, sorrow, calamity, the will of God, and—chiefly—death. Through careful discussions with the elders in the session, a beginning can be made whereby a Christian point of view may be formed concerning death and funeral customs, and consequently in times of emergency a common and proper stand will be disclosed spontaneously among the people. Indeed it is becoming customary in many churches for the session under the guidance of the minister to prepare a detailed statement of policy with regard to funeral regulations. It has been a real satisfaction to those responsible for such useful brochures that funeral directors themselves appreciate greatly this Christian orientation of a function of the church we have permitted to become mildly pagan.

Preparation for the Service

On the occasion of death and the inevitable sorrow accompanying it, the minister must acquit himself or herself effectively as a pastor. Helpfulness in the face of bereavement tests pastoral gifts and powers as nothing else can do. First of all, there is the visit to the family, which takes priority over every other responsibility the minister faces at this time. Here the minister must be patient and tactful, especially in homes where a throng of visitors—some sympathetic, some morbid—has gathered in a very brief space of time. By all means the family should assemble privately, and in unhurried conversation the minister will try to empathize with them in their sense of loss and match any sign of defeat or hostility with the note of Christian victory. Sometimes in particularly harrowing and tragic circumstances, the minister's presence means more than anything that might be said. Indeed there are times when one should remain quiet, for a sympathetic presence and the faith one represents may mean more to the bereaved than anything one can say. What is more, a minister is very likely to fail in his or her mission and never be remembered for helpful consolation if he or she arrives with little syllogisms on immortality all worked out beforehand and proceeds immediately to say a lengthy piece.

It could be that upon arrival the minister will find the plans for the funeral already worked out and settled. The minister should ask then if they have or want any suggestions regarding the service. Occasionally the family is so distraught that the minister must take full responsibility personally at this stage. On the other hand, in certain communities a thoughtful funeral director who is experienced in all kinds of unusual situations will arrange everything, except the service, to the benefit and satisfaction of all concerned. The wishes of the family must be adhered to and respected as far as possible, but every caution must be employed to keep all tributes to the deceased within a proper perspective and upon the level of good taste. When it appears that these preliminary matters have been taken care of adequately the minister should take his or her leave, but not without a brief prayer with the family.

The Service

Funeral services, except in some rural areas, are no longer held in private homes. In other areas, if there is a choice between the funeral chapel and the church, most arguments favor the latter, although local circumstances can influence the decision one way or the other. The procedures in the funeral chapel are quite simple and uniform and therefore the minister needs very little guidance except a suggestion or two from the director or undertaker, in fulfilling the assignment.

In a church service, however, both minister and funeral director should co-operate quietly and efficiently so that no confusion will mar what should be remembered by the family as a reverent experience. There are exceptional cases, however, when the funeral service is held in a church in another city or state, and therefore upon arrival something different from the usual preliminaries may be necessary. As the cortege arrives at the church, for example, the minister will meet the director and the pallbearers at the center door and precede the group down the main aisle to the chancel steps or wherever it is considered appropriate for the casket to be placed. The order of entry should be minister first, then pallbearers, followed by the family. The congregation should rise as a gesture of respect for the dead and of sympathy with the bereaved. The pallbearers will sit on the left, the family and relatives on the right. From this point the service begins and should incorporate a movement from the fact of human loss to our sense of victory through the risen and ascended Lord. A service lasting from twenty to thirty minutes may follow this format:

Sentences
Prayer (preferably a collect)
Hymn (only if choir or quartet is available to lead)
Lessons[5]
Prayers (if no eulogy, the prayer of thanksgiving may refer appropriately in passing to life and witness of the deceased)

[Eulogy—maybe in rare cases]
Hymn (at funeral chapel, usually no hymns are sung)
Benediction

The loss of a very distinguished citizen in church or government is sometimes an occasion for a brief and worthy tribute. In such cases, however, there should be no emotional demonstration, no profuse valediction, and certainly no attempt to argue the hope of immortality. Life and death must be seen in the light of the Christian faith, and this is more likely realized through simple sincerity and by means of good sense.

The service being over, the principals leave the church in the same order in which they entered.

The Burial

When the cortege arrives at the burial ground, the minister again precedes the principals and the casket and takes his or her stand at the head of the open grave. This is a time of strain and poignancy and therefore the prudent and discerning minister will be brief, especially if weather conditions are wet or cold. This service is more effective if it is done from memory.

Sentences (maybe Psalm 23 or John 11:25–26)
Words of Committal
Prayer (Newman's classic prayer beginning, "O Lord, support us all the day long . . ." is very appropriate)[6]
Benediction

The service being ended, the minister will take leave of the family. However, pastoral concern does not cease at this point. A friendship with the family at a deeper level has begun. A pastoral visit with them is made very soon and through personal interest and healing companionship the minister assists them in gathering up the broken strands of life's pattern and in beginning again upon the strength of the Christian hope. Some cases, however, will present unusual problems;

only the minister who has taken seriously the basic studies in pastoral counseling and has maintained generally an informed acquaintanceship with the best thinking in this field is likely to discern the underlying causes of distress and be able to give the Christian answer to them.

The following suggestions are made in order to assist in the wider acceptance of Christian funeral practices in our churches:

(1) In the event of death in the congregation the minister should be reached before any arrangements are made for the funeral service. It is reassuring for the family to receive wise counsel from their own minister and to feel that under such guidance everything will be carried out reverently and in accord with Christian customs.

(2) It should never be considered morbid or unsound for healthy Christian individuals to discuss with their ministers their personal wishes in the event of sudden death. These may reflect nothing more than general points of view, but if such were put in writing and deposited for safe keeping, the family would be relieved of undue emotional strain when they are least equipped to sustain it.

(3) The most appropriate place for the funeral service is the home church of the deceased, although some particular circumstances may require a funeral chapel or in rare cases a private home. Indeed, some ministers are recommending— with more than a little support—the practice of holding a private funeral and burial attended only by the family and a few relatives and friends. At a date soon after, a memorial service is held in the church, to which the congregation is invited.

(4) The intention of a funeral service is to surround the mourners with the strengthening fellowship of the church and to lift their attention from the sense of loss to the radiant assurance of eternal life through the risen Christ. There is no place, therefore, within the Christian context for emphasis upon costly embalming, "lifelike" appearance, and other occult arts. A body which had been the earthly temple of a

human personality, known and loved by his or her own people, is worthy of respect, but should never be made an object for "viewing" or for cheap and sentimental display before the public.

> Since the human body is merely the dwelling place of one's essential being and perishes at the time of death—a closed casket saves loved ones and friends unnecessary heartache and draws people away from an un-Christian conception of death.[7]

It is time for ministers and their sessions to become insistent upon this point and to demand that all pagan practices should cease.

(5) Abundant life is an expression of things eternal, not of the temporal. The custom of making a funeral the occasion for wealthy displays of expensive vaults, caskets, and floral offerings is contrary to the message and spirit of the New Testament. Many families in a time of emotional stress are apt to commit themselves to a financial outlay beyond their means, and in some cases they fall prey to the persuasiveness of an aggressive funeral director who is less than fair. The current revival of the use of a pall to cover the casket is commendable. It acts as a leveler in putting a temperate character upon ostentation, unintentional or otherwise.

(6) Each individual church should set up a memorial fund to which contributions may be made in lieu of floral tributes at funerals. It is becoming customary for bereaved persons to ask that such contributions be given to benevolent causes or to medical research. Some feel, however, that a wreath or a spray costs so little that no fund would be augmented noticeably by so small a gift.[8] However, any association—the Heart Fund or Cancer Society or Bible House—would be pleased to receive the receipts from the floral displays of all the funerals conducted in the United States on any *one* day. This custom may become more general when cremation is the accepted practice, as many hope will soon be the case.

(7) Ministers should not accept an honorarium for the funeral of a member of the congregation. In cases, however,

when a burial takes place in a distant city and somewhat extensive travel is involved, a thoughtful family will reimburse the minister for whatever expenses are incurred. The church should be available free of charge for all its members, but whenever the funeral of an outsider is held, some provision should be made for an organist, janitorial services, and, in cold weather, the heating of the sanctuary. Occasionally the deceased has indicated in his or her will that the officiating minister be paid, or in large cities where many non-church people are buried by whomsoever the funeral chapel director secures and a fee is automatically added, the clergy should have no hesitancy in accepting it and using it as need or conscience directs.

(8) No fraternal order, secret society, or brotherhood should be allowed to intrude upon the service which is rightfully the prerogative of the Christian church. In some places it is traditional for such organizations to recite their ritual at the graveside *after* the burial service of the church is ended. No minister should permit this arrangement. Much of this ritual is honorable and exalted, but is not necessarily Christian. The last word at an open grave must be spoken only by the church.

(9) During a funeral service the minister through the Christian word and witness will try to alleviate the grimness of death, yet he should not employ sentimental devices to hide its reality. One hears of all sorts of highly ornate and fluffy poetry being used in order to make death a matter of softness. Death is very real, and ministers are not entirely honest with themselves or their people if they fail to indicate that it entails "earth to earth, ashes to ashes, dust to dust." This spells out what we are saved *from*; the Christian message, however, declares that the life's center of gravity is beyond the grave; that is what we are saved *to*. Lowell H. Zuch writes, "The Christian faith has never lost sight of the reality and inevitability of death. . . . [Christianity recalls] that resurrection for the Christian as well as for Christ could be a reality only after faithful submission to suffering, decay, and

death.''[9] At the funeral of King George VI of Great Britain, the Archbishop of Canterbury did not attempt to gloss over the human and earthly side of life for fear of obscuring the heavenly. He recited, "For as much as it hath pleased Almighty God to take unto himself the soul of our brother here departed, we therefore commit his body to the ground, *earth* to earth, *ashes* to ashes, *dust* to dust . . ."

(10) No occasion presents greater difficulty to the minister than the funeral of a suicide. In this instance the wishes of the family must take priority. For the minister the problem is somewhat lessened through the realization that our ministry is never to the departed but to the bereaved. One dare not be legalistic. It is not our role to judge the dead, nor to intimate that any one of God's creatures is forever lost. The emphasis should be upon the nature of God's will, and upon the hope that even those things which seem to defy his purposes for us can be woven by his grace into the fabric of life in order that something positive may result.

(11) The traditional passages of Scripture used at funerals are among some of the finest devotional utterances ever framed by the human mind and voice; for example, Psalms 23 and 139; John 14:1–9, 27; Revelation 21:1–4; 22:1–5. No minister should ever use hymns, prayers, or poems that are very inferior in language and thought to these writings. There is a place for both read and extemporary prayers in a funeral service. Obviously none of us can match the lone sentiment of Newman's classic prayer,

> O Lord, support us all the day long of this troublous life, until the shadows lengthen and the evening comes, and the busy world is hushed, and the fever of life is over, and our work is done. Then in thy mercy grant us a safe lodging, and a holy rest, and peace at the last; through Jesus Christ our Lord. Amen.

Yet no one should presume on the other hand that prayers of thanksgiving and intercession on this responsible occasion can be merely the tawdry expression of the fragmentary musings of the moment. There is also the music and the hymns.

We must have done with "Beautiful Isle of Somewhere" and select instead those hymns which are the expression of a mature theology and of sober courage, such as "For all the saints, who from their labors rest" (Sine Nomine), "Ten thousand times ten thousand" (Alford), "The Lord's my Shepherd" (Martyrdom), "O God of Bethel" (Salzburg), "Unto the hills" (Sandon), or "Peace, perfect peace" (Pax Tecum). A pamphlet, "Music for Church Funerals,"[10] contains a useful list of suggested organ music, anthems, and solos for funeral and memorial services.

(12) Every minister should keep a funeral file where random clippings and jottings, quotations and poetry, prayers and helpful suggestions, are kept in order of subject or topic. Also there are prayers which every minister writes personally for an occasion when the enormity of the loss or the poignancy of the sorrow has staggered the mind, and the words seem to issue from the fountains of the heart. These ought to be preserved, because no later time can recapture the word patterns of the hour in which as never before a minister realized himself or herself to be a helper of the helpless only by God's help.

LITERATURE

Blackwood, A. W. *The Funeral*. Philadelphia: The Westminister Press, 1942.

Cabot, R. C., and Dicks, R. L. *The Art of Ministering to the Sick*. New York: The Macmillan Co., 1936.

Halsey, Jesse. *A Living Hope: Suggestions for Funeral Services*. Nashville: Abingdon Press, 1932.

Irion, Paul E. *The Funeral and the Mourners*. Nashville: Abingdon Press, 1954.

————. *Cremation*. Philadelphia: Fortress Press, 1968.

Messersmith, L. H. "The Minister's Relation to the Funeral." Unpublished B. D. thesis. Federated Theological Faculty, University of Chicago.

Mitford, Jessica. *The American Way of Death*. New York: Simon & Schuster, 1963.

Wallis, Charles L. *The Funeral Encyclopedia*. New York: Harper and Brothers, 1953.

LITURGIES AND PRAYERS

The Book of Common Worship. The United Presbyterian Church, pp. 193–214, 1946 edition.

The Worshipbook. The United Presbyterian Church. pp. 71–86, 1972 edition.

Noyes, Morgan P. *Prayers for Services.* New York: Charles Scribner's Sons, 1934.

Biddle, Perrry H. *Abingdon Funeral Manual.* Nashville: Abingdon Press, 1976.

7
The Christian Year

"The Christian Year is the ordered effort of the church to represent in its annual worship the whole body of Christian truth—all of divine revelation in the Scriptures, in the historic church, and in human experience."[1] This, according to Charles H. Heimsath, is the intention of the Christian Year.

I

Origin and Meaning of Sunday

Historically speaking, Sunday has been the foundation of the entire structure of the Christian Year. However, Sunday, or "The Lord's Day" as the Scots call it, is not the same thing as the Jewish Sabbath. In the Jewish calendar the days of the week were not named, but numbered; the seventh day was the Sabbath, which comes from the root *shabath,* meaning "to cease." Originally it was designated as a day of rest from all labor, and even from early Babylonian relations this weekly practice distinguished the Jews from the neighboring nations and tribes. Indeed the Jews believed it went "back in an uninterrupted seven-day cycle to the first Sabbath described in Genesis 2:1–3."[2] Friday (or the sixth day) was always the "day of preparation," as in Mark 15:42, "And when evening had come, since it was the day of Preparation [παρασκευή], that is, the day before the sabbath."

In the Christian era, however, the *first* day of the week became the day of rest and subsequently the day of worship (Acts 20:7; 1 Corinthians 16:2). The genesis of this tradition may be seen through references gathered from biblical and other early Christian writings. In Revelation 1:10, for example, the term "Lord's day" appears. Then, in *The Didache*, a fuller phrase, "The Lord's Day of the Lord," is used. In Justin Martyr's *Apology* (circa A.D. 148–161), we find the word "Sunday" for the first time: "On the day called Sunday, all who live in cities or in the country gather together to one place."[3] It may be added that the Puritans unfortunately equated the Jewish term *Sabbath* with the Christian *Sunday* and hence this incorrect designation was carried over into *The Westminster Confession of Faith* in the heading of Chapter XXIII, "Of Religious Worship and the Sabbath Day." In the writings of Pliny (circa A.D. 111–113), reference is made to the story of the Resurrection being read "On all Lord's Days" throughout the year. And then Constantine in his edict, A.D. 321, decreed, "All judges, city people and craftsmen shall rest on the venerable day of the Sun."[4]

Very early, moreover, Sunday as the first day of the week became associated with the Resurrection. In Mark 16:2 (K.J.V.), we read, "And very early on the first day of the week they went to the tomb when the sun had risen." In the second century there seemed to be more conviction about the matter, for in the *Epistle of Barnabas* (circa A.D. 131) we find:

> The present sabbaths are not acceptable to me, but that which I have made, in which I will give rest to all things and make the beginning of an eighth day, that is the beginning of another world. Wherefore we also celebrate with gladness the eighth day in which Jesus also rose from the dead . . .[5]

Again Justin Martyr in his *Apology* writes: "Sunday is the day on which we all hold our common assembly, because it is the first day on which God, having wrought a change in darkness and matter, made the world; and Jesus Christ our Savior on the same day rose from the dead." One of the best known and most descriptive statements of early Christian practices on a stated day comes from Pliny the Younger who sent a message from Bithynia (circa A.D. 112) to the emperor requesting directions how he might deal with the Christians:

They affirmed, however, the whole of their guilt, or their error, was, that they were in the habit of meeting on a certain fixed day before it was light [*stato die ante lucem*], when they sang in alternate verses a hymn to Christ, as to a god, and bound themselves by a solemn oath, not to any wicked deeds, but never to commit any fraud, theft or adultery, never to falsify their word, nor deny a trust when they should be called upon to deliver it up; after which it was their custom to separate, and then reassemble to partake of food—but food of an ordinary and innocent kind.[6]

Over a century later Cyprian of Carthage (circa A.D. 250) wrote, "We celebrate the resurrection of the Lord in the morning." The link between Sunday and the Resurrection is illustrated best from the next century by a document published in Rome in 1887 called *Peregrinatio*, which gave an account of a pilgrimage made from Spain during A.D. 393–396 by Etheria, a member of a sisterhood in Galicia. She described the early Sunday service in this way:

On the Lord's Day, the whole multitude assembles before cockcrow. . . . Now as soon as the first cock has crowed, the Bishop arrives and enters the cave at the Anastasis [the sanctuary of the Resurrection]. . . . After these three psalms and three prayers are ended . . . the Bishop, standing within the rails, takes the book of the Gospel, and proceeding to the door, himself reads the (narrative of the) Resurrection of the Lord.[7]

This service was held each Sunday prior to the central service at daybreak which included "the reading and preaching of the Word and the celebration of the Sacrament."[8]

Of equal importance to what was done is the spirit and temper of these services. The theme was joy and spiritual triumph. Each Sunday was indeed "a little Easter." Its message was Christ Risen. Not that these people overlooked the Cross; they saw the Cross *through* the Resurrection. Not only were these Sunday services marked with gladness, but it was a glad Thanksgiving. The sacrament was εὐχαριστία—a Thanksgiving—and in its words of remembrance *(anamnesis)* the recital of Jesus' sorrow, suffering, and death was overarched by a note of victory, "Jesus Christ is Lord" (Romans 10:9; Philippians 2:9–11). Dom Gregory Dix has said, "Sunday marked the periodical manifestation in time of the reality of eternal redemption in Christ. As such it was an *anamnesis* of the resurrection which had manifested to His first disciples the Lord's conquest of sin and death and time and all this world-order."[9] This became the character of Sunday and its worship, and in the first generation of the church's life the final separation of the Jewish Sabbath and the Christian Sunday took place.

The scope of this remembrance, however, did not remain constricted in its focus upon Christ's death and resurrection only. Through the centuries other events of the story of God's great redemptive revelation to humanity were added until, in Heimsath's phrase, "the whole body of Christian truth" was incorporated within the compass of the church's celebration.

II

Jewish and Roman Precedents

Now the origin of the idea of the Christian Year came from Jewish traditions, from those celebrations which formed the basic framework of their religious life. Again the Sabbath was the pivotal day. There were three great annual feasts that brought the Jews to Jerusalem: Feast of Passover, Feast of Pentecost, and Feast of Tabernacles. The Passover was celebrated on the fourteenth day of the month Nisan (about March 21) and continued for eight days; it was associated with the spring planting of grain and a commemoration of the delivery of the children of Israel from bondage in Egypt. Pentecost came fifty days later when the first harvest was gathered in. Originally it was known as "Feast of Weeks," occurring seven weeks after the first planting, but it acquired eventually the name $\pi\epsilon\nu\tau\eta\kappa\sigma\tau\acute{\eta}$ from Greek-speaking Jews. It continued for eight days also and was marked by thanksgiving for the first fruits of the ground. Then late in the autumn the Feast of

Tabernacles was observed in recognition of the ancient journey through the wilderness and of the final harvest. Its spirit was somewhat similar to the English "Harvest Home" and the American and Canadian "Thanksgiving." Other celebrations of the Jewish calendar include the Feast of Trumpets and Feast of Lights, and such "high holy days" as New Year *(Rosh Hashanah)* and Day of Atonement *(Yom Kippur)*. All these celebrations were current at the time of Jesus' ministry and even for many years after the Resurrection, Christians who had been pious Jews continued their ancient customs as well as the new Christian festivals.

For the Hebrews the measurement of time and the pattern of the calendar were determined by the moon. Indeed the word "month" came from "moon" and was the measure of the time from one new moon to the next, approximately 29½ days. This meant that a lunar year, consisting of 12 lunar months, formed a period of 354 days, shorter by 11 days than the solar year, used by the Romans. Later, however, Julius Caesar had the solar calendar revised and in 45 B.C. the Julian system, which was to last sixteen centuries, was introduced. It was not, however, without its disadvantages, especially the nuisance of its gaining a day every so many years and hence such festivals as Christmas and Easter moved gradually toward the wrong seasons. Finally, in 1582, Pope Gregory XIII framed a time structure with the idea of leap years and so constituted it that no appreciable variation should occur in 20,000 years. This system was slow to take hold, but by the eighteeneth century it had become general in Europe, Britain, and America.

Scarcely any work had been done on chronology until the sixth century when a monk, Dionysius the Little, marked the year of Jesus' birth as "one." Everything before this date was Ante Christum (before Christ) and everything afterward was Anno Domini (in the year of our Lord). Later the former was anglicized to B.C. and the latter is recognized and used almost solely by the abbreviation A.D.

III

The Christian Calendar

Advent (four Sundays)
Christmas Day (December 25)
After Christmas (one or two Sundays)
Epiphany (as many as six Sundays)
Ash Wednesday
Lent (40 days excluding Sundays)
Passion Sunday
Palm Sunday
Holy Week
   Maundy Thursday
   Good Friday
Easter Day
Eastertide (40 days)
Ascension Day (always on Thursday)
Pentecost
Trinity Sunday
Sundays after Trinity (or in some churches "after Pentecost")

Every denomination, country, and local situation has its own catalogue of special observances, many of which have little warrant in a Christian calendar, although a limited number have lost their secular edge through constant association with religious causes. The most permissible ones are: Bible Sunday, New Year's Eve, New Year's Day, Universal Week of Prayer, World Day of Prayer, Independence Day, Labor Sunday, Rally Day, World-Wide Communion Sunday, and Thanksgiving Day.

Advent: The name comes from the Latin verb *advenio,* "to come," and in the Christian Year it refers to the coming of Jesus Christ. Advent, however, has a double significance: it looks forward and backward. It recalls the coming of Christ as the child of Bethlehem and his coming again to judge in power and victory. Indeed Advent is an introduction not only to Christmas but also to the whole cycle of the Christian Year. Its message challenges us to fulfill John the Baptist's exhortation, "Prepare the way of the Lord" (Matthew 3:3). This call therefore implies self-examination: are we ready to receive him? Hence the mood of Advent is repentance and self-examination. The liturgical color is purple or violet which by its quiet, subdued hue has become associated traditionally with penitence.

Historically the observance of Advent goes back to the sixth century, but these early references indicate a variety of duration from two to six Sundays. It appears that this festival originated in Spain in the fifth century and reached Italy in the sixth and from there became a custom of the whole church. An examination of ancient lectionaries reveals tables of lessons for a two-Sunday, five-Sunday, and more generally a six-Sunday Advent. The Council of Tours (A.D. 565) referred to a penitential period of six weeks prior to Christmas Eve. Eventually, Gregory the Great set the period as four Sundays, although it is interesting to note that in *The Book of Common Prayer* the last Sunday after Trinity or Pentecost has the Advent theme. In the Western churches Advent is recognized as the four Sundays prior to Christmas Day. The Anglican Church provides a structure of meaning for the season by designating a theme for each Sunday: (1) a plea for God's help in casting off the works of darkness and putting on the armor of light; (2) Bible Sunday; (3) the ministry of the church and its responsibility to proclaim the coming of the Redeemer; (4) a call to live worthily in view of the visitation from on high, with special reference to the character of John the Baptist. Generally Presbyterian preachers use these Sundays for a series of sermons on the significance of the Incarnation and its influence upon the meaning of Christmas and our celebration of it.

Christmas: The most popular of all the Christian festivals is the season of Christmas. Its removal would create a tremendous vacuum in our religious and cultural life. The name itself, an English contraction of the phrase Christ's Mass, did not become general until the twelfth century, although there were other earlier designations, such as the Feast of the Nativity, *Dies Natalis* (Latin), and *Noël* (French). The season lasts for a period of twelve days between December 25 and January 6 and may contain either one or two Sundays, depending upon the day of the week upon which Christmas Day falls. The message of Christmas is basically the meaning of the word *Incarnation* which comes from the Latin *caro* ("flesh") and of *Immanuel* ("God with us"). The Nicene Creed puts it, "was incarnate by the Holy Ghost of the Virgin Mary, and was made man." Matthew and Luke in their Gospels surround the event with nativity stories of unexcelled beauty, and John and Paul express its significance in comprehensive statements such as John 3:16 and 2 Corinthians 5:19.

As a specific festival Christmas was unknown in the church for the first two centuries of the Christian era. This was due mainly to the fact that during the early spread of Christianity the emphasis of the church was upon the ministry and mission of Christ climaxed by his death and resurrection.[10] Also, there was the disposition in early times to regard the celebration of birthdays as pagan. "The martyrs," according to Hauck, ". . . were remembered on the dates of their martyrdom rather than upon the dates of their birth . . . the heavenly birthday was much more imporant than the earthly one."[11] The first intimation of a celebration of Christ's birth came out of Egypt about A.D. 200 and Rome in A.D. 336. It was not until the fourth century that December 25 was set as the accepted date for this festival. It is interesting to note that an old pagan festival was held on this same date as recognition of the winter solstice when the sun began to return from its autumnal decline. St. Chrysostom reported that Pope Julius I (Bishop of Rome, A.D. 337–352) was probably responsible for establishing December 25 as the birthdate of Christ. For Christmas the liturgical color is white, signifying joy, thanksgiving, and victory.

Epiphany: Deriving its name from the Greek word ἐπιφάνια ("manifestation" or "showing forth"), this is one of the oldest festivals of the Christian church, antedating Christmas itself. It was observed in Asia Minor and Egypt as early as the second century. Its season is from January sixth to Ash Wednesday, and since its length depends upon the movable festival of Easter it can contain as many as six Sundays. The original significance of Epiphany for the Eastern church was Jesus' baptism by John; for the Western church, it recalled the visit of the Magi and the "manifestation" of Christ to the Gentiles. For some time there had been a controversy between Eastern and Western points of view whether the emphasis should be upon Christmas (the Incarnation) or Epiphany (the Baptism of Jesus). The rise of the christological debates, especially Arianism, was determinative in making Christmas the chief celebration in the West because of its emphasis upon the Incarnation. Epiphany, therefore, came gradually to have several meanings: Christ's showing to the Wise Men symbolized his revelation to the Gentiles as the Light of the World; this manifestation stresses the missionary cause and the need of making all peoples the children of light. Today in many Protestant churches Epiphany gathers up several events that are more or less closely related chronologically: the Wise Men, the baptism, and Jesus' first miracle at the wedding at Cana, although in recent decades the Magi have somehow been moved up and are joined with the vigil at the manger of Bethlehem. This bears out the opinion that our hymns have had an extensive effect upon our religious thought, especially the patterns of our festivals, for example, Christopher Wordsworth's "Songs of Thankfulness and Praise" and John H. Hopkin's carol, "We Three Kings of Orient Are." Note the close association of events in Wordsworth's lines:

> Songs of thankfulness and praise,
> Jesus, Lord, to thee we raise,
> Manifested by the Star
> To the sages from afar;
> Branch of royal David's stem
> In thy birth at Bethlehem;
> Anthems to be thee addressed
> God in man made manifest.

The liturgical color for the Feast of Epiphany is white, while for the rest of the season the color is green. White symbolizes joy and light, while green, the color of nature, signifies the universal redemption Christ brought to the world.

Lent: This season begins with Ash Wednesday and continues for forty days and six Sundays prior to Easter Day. It is a period of discipline but not necessarily of a negative character. As someone has said, "Lent consists in doing something, not in merely doing without something." The genesis of Lent appears to have been associated with a period of discipline, reflections, and abstinence in imitation of Christ's self-denial and in preparation for the holy celebration of Easter. But since every Sunday was a "little Easter" and every Friday a day of fasting in memory of Calvary, it was comparatively easy to require a longer period of discipline as appropriate provision for Easter Day. By the third century the period was six days. The earliest record of a forty-day period was in the fourth century when Athanasius urged the people of Alexandria to fast, and in a reference in Canon V of the Council of Nicaea (A.D. 325). By the eighth century Ash Wednesday was generally observed as the beginning of Lent. Also, since Sunday was traditionally a "little Easter," the six Sundays are not counted in the Lenten fast and are therefore separate from the forty days. Hence we say the first or second Sunday *in* Lent. The word "Lent" comes from the Old English *lencten*, meaning "the lengthening" of the days in spring.

The day before Lent is known as Shrove Tuesday. Although it has never been part of the church's calendar, yet from earliest times it has been an occasion when people confessed their sins and were "shriven" (an archaic form for "absolve"). After confession and as a final feast before the beginning of the long period of Lenten abstinence, in some areas a carnival is held, such as the Mardi Gras (Fat Tuesday) in New Orleans. Also among some peoples milk and eggs as well as meat, were excluded from their diet and therefore Shrove Tuesday was an occasion to fill up on pancakes and later to feast on eggs on Easter Day.

Ash Wednesday gets its name from Old Testament times when "sackcloth and ashes" were symbols of repentance. In Roman Catholic churches, the priest takes the ashes of some of the palm branches consecrated the previous year and marks the forehead of each kneeling penitent at the altar rail and repeats in Latin, *Memento, homo, quia pulvis es et in pulverem reverteris* ("Remember, man, that thou art dust; and unto dust thou shalt return").

In the Anglican Church, each Sunday in Lent has its separate designation, but generally in Presbyterian churches, only Passion Sunday and Palm Sunday are singled out by special themes. The former reminds us of the nearness of the crucifixion and the sorrow of Calvary; the latter celebrates the triumphal entry into Jerusalem and formally opens the observance of Holy Week. During the next few days the church follows closely the movements of Jesus as tradition outlines them. Monday: cleansing of the temple; Tuesday: verbal conflict with his enemies; Wednesday: day of silence and retreat in Bethany; Thursday: final conversations with his disciples; Friday: the crucifixion; Saturday: his body lay in the tomb. Maundy Thursday takes its name from the new "mandate" or "commandment" Jesus gave to his disciples to "love one another" and from the institution of the Last Supper to be done "in remembrance of me." Special services have marked Good Friday from as early as the fourth century. Three-hour services began with the Roman church in the seventeenth century and now have become general in most Protestant denominations also. The origin of the name "Good" Friday is obscure; some scholars conclude that it is a corruption of "God's" Friday.

Lent ends officially at noon on Saturday. In the Anglican tradition it has been usually an occasion for baptisms, in keeping with the theological emphasis that we are "buried with Christ in his death" or as the Collect reads "as we are baptized into the death of Thy blessed Son," so grant that "through the grave, and gate of death, we may pass to our joyful resurrection." For Lent the liturgical color is violet, which symbolizes the mood of the season. On Good Friday in highly liturgical traditions the altar is stripped, candles are not lighted, and the cross is veiled in black.

Easter: Easter Day (there is no such term as "Easter Sunday") signals the beginning of the festival of the Resurrection which continues for forty days, corresponding to the period Christ was manifest upon earth before the Ascension. Easter is known as a "movable" feast, that is, its date varies from year to year and, what is more, it regulates the time and length of many other festivals of the Christian Year. Indeed, as Frank Wilson comments, "Easter is the axis on which the Christian Year revolves."[12]

The date of Easter was a controversial point between Eastern and Western Christendom for some time prior to the Council of Nicaea. Each side felt that both the death and resurrection of Christ should be commemorated at the time of the year when they actually occurred, but they were in disagreement whether this date might be Sunday or a weekday. For example, the time of the crucifixion was identified closely with the Jewish Passover which fell on the fourteenth day of the Jewish month Nisan. But if this date did not fall on Friday, the West kept the following Friday and celebrated Easter two days later, on Sunday. The East, however, observed the death of Christ on the fourteenth regardless of the day of the week. To resolve the dispute the issue was given to a group of neutral experts in Alexandria, Egypt, who came up with the formula, later adopted at Nicaea, which set the celebration of the Resurrection upon Sunday. Easter Day is calculated to be the first Sunday following the first full moon after the spring equinox, March twenty-first. The Greek name for Easter is *Pascha;* the Italian, *Pasqua;* and the English comes from *Eostre,* the name of a Teutonic goddess of Spring. It is a season of joy and triumph; it marks the summit of the Christian Year. The liturgical color is white.

Ascension: Ascension Day comes on the fortieth day after Easter and since this is invariably a weekday, its significance has suffered from lack of consideration. Originally Ascension-tide was part of the season between Easter and Pentecost, but by the fourth century it was given a separate identity. It is seen now as the final act in God's drama of redemption, and it marks the completion of Christ's ministry upon the earth. The season continues for ten days and corresponds to the length of time the disciples waited in Jerusalem for the gift of the Holy Spirit which came at Pentecost. From Advent to Ascension-tide we have Christ presented to us in his ministry upon earth; from Pentecost onwards, his eternal ministry is contin-ued through his Body, the church. Again, the liturgical color is white.

Pentecost: This festival had its roots in the ancient Jewish Feast of Weeks, a celebration of the first harvest, seven weeks after the spring sowing of the grain. In Exodus 23:16 we read, "You shall keep the feast of harvest, of the first fruits of your labor, of what you sow in the field." (See also Numbers 28:26–31; Leviticus 23:15–22; Deuteronomy 16:9–12.) For the Christian, however, Pentecost has a twofold significance quite independent from the Jewish tradition. It commemo-rates that stirring event in Acts 2 when two things occurred: the Holy Spirit came in fulfillment of Christ's promise to his disciples and the Christian church was launched upon its world mission. In England this festival has been known tradi-tionally as Whitsuntide. It was a special day for baptisms and the candidates were robed in white; hence "White Sunday," which was later contracted to Whitsuntide. This season lasts seven days and the liturgical color is red, reminiscent of the tongues of flame that rested upon the apostles on the original Day of Pentecost.

Trinity: Whitsunday is followed by Trinity Sunday, which came late in the calendar of the Christian church. The need for greater emphasis upon the doctrine of the Holy Trinity and the teaching it implies became most acute when the church encountered the various heresies of the early centu-ries. Yet it was not until the tenth century that its recognition was more or less general, and not until the twelfth that it was adopted in England. This season covers the period of six months between Pentecost and Advent, which can contain from twenty-two to twenty-seven Sundays, depending upon the date of Easter. These Sundays are designated by English and European churches as "after Trinity," while in America they are sometimes called "after Pentecost." The theme and purpose of the season is an attempt to keep God's commandments and so "please thee, both in will and deed."[13] Spiritual nourishment derived from observance of the first half of the Christian Year must yield fruit in righteous living. Or, as Wilson writes:

> Christianity is more than an idea, a philosophy or a theory. It is a way of life. Grounded as it is in the historic facts of our Lord's life and ministry, it strains for action in the daily living of Christian people. . . . To believe in Christ demands that something be done about it. Pointing the way is the function of the Trinity season.[14]

IV

Values in the Christian Year

One of the characteristics of the contemporary liturgical renewal is a fresh emphasis upon the value of the Christian Year after it had suffered an eclipse in the Reformed churches for some centuries. In some quarters there is a tendency to deplore this new emphasis as an upsurge of ceremonial or as an attempt to stereotype our program of worship through a rigidly recurring system. But none of these negative rejoinders can cancel out the many positive advantages that accrue from a sensible and well-balanced observance of the Christian Year. The choice is plainly between the dignity of the Christian Year and the continuance of disorder. Promotional schemes from the official headquarters of the denomination vie with local and civic groups to claim the church's Sundays for the temporary hobby someone happens to be riding, and hence we get a multicolored mash of religion and secularism that has lowered the level of Christian witness through worship. The urgent need, however, is for worship practices that are theologically meaningful and biblically oriented. The Christian Year provides most easily that framework in which the program of the church's worship can be structured according to the great story of God's coming to humanity in Christ and the wonderful events of his earthly life. As now constituted, the year's worship in many Presbyterian churches is a higgledy-piggledy presentation of some festivals—such as Christmas and Easter—with the others discarded in favor of World Order Day, Election Day, Student Recognition Day, National YMCA Week, Campfire Girls Founder's Day, Soil Stewardship Week, Pensions Sunday, Mother's Day, and so on.[15] Is it not time to discover that the Apostles' Creed and the program of the Christian Year are linked together, the former giving a pattern to the latter?

This brings us to one nagging problem peculiar to American church life today. The annual program of activities of most Presbyterian churches begins in mid-September and concludes with Children's Day in June. The whole vacation period from mid-June to mid-September is a void; ministers and congregations are in a prolonged recess and no attempt is made to retain consistency of theme or witness when attendance is a fraction of its regular size. Depleted choirs, elderly folk, and visiting preachers simply "carry on." In some extremes the church's program begins actually at Advent and ends at Easter.

One of the most thoughtful and scholarly attempts to cope with this situation is found in *The Christian Year and Lectionary Reform*,[16] by A. Allan McArthur. He was cognizant of the fact that the Roman pattern might not be completely suitable "as an ideal for the Protestant Church in the mid-twentieth century," and he went on to point out that when the Christian Year begins with Advent, we commence actually with the *second* article of the Apostles' Creed. "God the Father Almighty, Maker of heaven and earth" was overlooked and "Jesus Christ his only Son, our Lord" became the initial affirmation. Hence, he urged that we should take the six sections of the Creed as follows: (1) Creation and Providence: (2) Incarnation; (3) Ministry and Passion; (4) Resurrection, Ascension, and Second Coming; (5) Church and Christian Life; (6) Christian Hope. Prior to Advent, therefore, would be a season focusing upon the revelation of God the Father in which the themes, readings, and sermons for six Sundays would comprise the Festival of Creation. The Church Year would begin then with World Communion the first Sunday in October and the six Sundays of the Festival of Creation that follow would bring us to Advent. In the Church and Christian Life season, there would be possibly fifteen Sundays (after Pentecost), leaving the last two Sundays of September for a celebration of the Christian Hope.

A similar pattern was projected originally in the new *Lectionary for the Christian Year* by the Joint Committee on Worship of the Presbyterian Church, U.S. and the United Presbyterian Church, U.S.A. in 1966. The traditional period from Advent through Christmas, Epiphany, Lent, Easter, to Ascensiontide was called "God the Son." Then the period from Pentecost to World Communion was the season of "God the Spirit." From World Communion to the last Sunday before Advent was a new seasonal modification and was named "God the Father." In this pattern an effort was made "to ensure that the church year will witness clearly to the full-rounded trinitarian affirmation of the church."[17] This arrangement, however, was abandoned—which was unfortunate—in order to conform, along with the other mainline Protestant denominations with the new post-Vatican II lectionary of the Roman Catholic Church (cf. Preface to *A Lectionary*, The Consultation on Church Union, 1974, pp. 1, 2).

To conclude, we may sum up the benefits that can be gained from careful following and adaptation of the Christian Year.

(1) A complete gospel is presented. Heresy creeps in when one part is emphasized at the expense of all the others. A whole gospel makes for a well-balanced spiritual life.

(2) The materials of the Christian Year include all the great beliefs of the church universal. Despite opinions to the contrary, modern congregations are eager to know what can be believed most surely in a time when many traditional religious tenets are either watered down or discredited altogether. A careful exploration of the doctrines of God, man, grace, the church, sin, future life, etc., is more likely to be done regularly and with up-to-date thinking if the discipline of the Christian Year is allowed to be exercised.

(3) Emphasis upon the Bible is structured with proper balance. With the increasing ignorance of the Bible among Protestants it is essential now that some scheme be framed for regular reading of the Scripture. The *Lectionary* covers the Bible in two years, and although no one is expected to adhere slavishly to its sequence, yet ministers can plan worship more meaningfully if they glance at its outline regularly. In the hands of the people a lectionary is useful for Bible readings at home.

(4) A sense of tradition is enhanced and appropriated. Too many worshipers, especially in the "free" churches, lack a sense of historical perspective and a grasp of their denominational tradition. Christian denominations hold in common scores of martyrs, missionaries, preachers, and saints, many of whom were pivotal figures in the great turning points in ecclesiastical history and about whom modern folk—even good church members—are ignorant. The Christian Year recalls the whole panorama of the Church Catholic through the ages and broadens the horizons of those Protestants who think Christianity began at the Reformation.

(5) Within the total program of the local church, the Christion Year is indispensable to the method and content of religious education. Among the Jews the religious calendar, with its great program of festivals, was intended to educate each succeeding generation. Read Exodus 12:26: "And when your children say to you, 'What do you mean by this service?' you shall say, 'It is the sacrifice of the LORD'S passover, for he passed over the houses of the people of Israel in Egypt, when

he slew the Egyptians but spared our houses.'" (See also Genesis 18:19; Deuteronomy 6:6–7; Psalm 78:3–7.) The Jews realized that only through constant reiteration of a certain body of religious knowledge would it be transmitted successfully from one generation to another.

(6) Recognition of the Christian Year assures the benefits of planned preaching. Today ministers must not fail to see the need for careful planning of their sermon subjects and themes. They are blind if they do not recognize that all of us are most free when we follow an ordered routine. As any minister plans for the major seasons of the Christian Year he or she develops whole areas of Christian thought and thereby is saved from disjointed and frantic hand-to-mouth pulpit presentations. Preaching that is planned purposefully educates both minister and congregation. Therefore, there is less danger of following one's own pet interests or riding favorite hobbies. Ethical, social, national, civic, and evangelistic issues will be dealt with in good proportion and within the framework of a total gospel emphasis.

LITERATURE

Fuller, R. H. *Preaching the New Lectionary.* Collegeville, Minn.: The Liturgical Press, 1974.

Gibson, George M. *The Story of the Christian Year.* Nashville: Abingdon Press, 1945.

McArthur, A.A. *The Evolution of the Christian Year.* London: SCM Press, 1953.

————. *The Christian Year and Lectionary Reform.* London: SCM Press, 1958.

Nocent, Adrian. *The Liturgical Year.* Collegeville, Minn.: The Liturgical Press, 1977.

Vol. 1: Advent, Christmas, Epiphany.

Vol. 2: Lent, Holy Week.

Vol. 3: The Easter Season.

Vol. 4: Sundays in Ordinary Time.

Rordorf, Willy. *Sunday.* Philadelphia: The Westminster Press, 1968.

Proclamation: Aids for Interpreting the Lessons of the Church Year. Philadelphia: Fortress Press, 1975.

LECTIONARIES

The St. Andrew's Lectionary of Bible Lessons for Use in Services of Public Worship. Second edition published concurrently in 1944 by The Church of Scotland, The Methodist Church, The Congregational Union, and The Presbyterian Church of England.

The Book of Common Worship. United Presbyterian Church, U.S.A., pp. 376–388, 1946 edition.

The Worshipbook. The United Presbyterian Church, U.S.A., pp. 135–175, 1972 edition.

A Lectionary. Consultation on Church Union. Princeton, N.J., 1974.

PRAYERS

Prayers for the Christian Year. Church of Scotland. London: Oxford University Press, 1952.

Coloquhoun, Frank. *Parish Prayers.* London: Hodder & Stoughton, 1967.

————. *Contemporary Parish Prayers.* London: Hodder & Stoughton, 1975.

Williams, Dick. *Prayers for Today's Church.* London: CPAS Publications, 1972.

8

The Proprieties
of the Sanctuary

Minister and Choir Director

The Directory for Worship states:[1]

> God has provided that men may give glory to him in the corporate singing of hymns and psalms. The true choir for such singing is the entire congregation. Where there is an auxiliary choir the members thereof should be drawn as far as practicable from the congregation itself. When the choir sings alone it is representing the congregation, just as on occasion the minister may pray alone, representing the congregation. The main function of the choir, however, is to act as a part of the congregation, offering its special gifts to God so that the full congregation may sing more faithfully and share more fully in the service.

> Where there is a choir director, although he will bring to his task special gifts of competence and training, he will consult with the minister, who, representing the authority of the session, is responsible for the direction and leading of the service. Hymns and other music should center not upon the worshiper but upon him who is worshiped.

Fortunate is that church whose minister and choir director hold each other in mutual respect and co-operate in making the act of worship a worthy offering to God. Examples of complex situations are endless. Many of them, however, could be forestalled through a spirit of understanding and tact or the use of sober thought in preference to an emotional skirmish. The blame in most cases cannot be laid upon any one person, but from the perspective of the pulpit "one of the pitfalls every minister should avoid is a closed mind toward church music."[2]

The majority of potential misunderstandings can be avoided by setting up an efficient and responsible Worship Committee under the supervision of the session. Although this committee is appointed by the session and may consist entirely of members of the session, sometimes other competent and musically informed members of the congregation are co-opted to serve, even in simply an advisory capacity. The duties of such a committe will vary according to local situations, and certainly their responsibilities will be more complex in a church of 3000 members than in one of 300, although in all cases the basic issues can be surprisingly similar. Their supervision may include the following:

(1) They should exercise jurisdiction over the quality of music used in the service of worship.

(2) They will be expected to make recommendations to the session regarding personnel, such as prospective soloists, organist, or director.

(3) Special musical services may be cleared through them, so that several organizations do not schedule similar events for the same Sunday.

(4) They should act as a liaison group in negotiating salaries and other benefits with the trustees.

(5) Ordinarily a congregation should use the authorized hymnbook of the denomination. This committee, however, may initiate discussion whenever new editions of any hymnbook are projected and may even make formal recommendations through the session to the denominational authorities.

(6) Whenever necessary, this committee may request the purchase or repair of musical instruments used in any act of worship, such as organs, pianos, and carillon.

In short, this committee, if well chosen, can fulfill an important function in maintaining a high level of quality, not only of performance in acts of worship, but of mind and spirit in the many discussions that must go on "behind the scenes." They can be a fair and sympathetic court of appeal for either organist or soloist who feels that he or she has been willfully wronged. At the same time, however, a prudent minister will scotch a rift before it goes that far and by quiet negotiation may be able to settle grievances promptly and set matters aright.

Every minister, moreover, will aim to co-operate closely with the choir director in the following ways:

(1) There should be a mutually acceptable policy between minister and choir director regarding the type of hymn to be used in the regular services of worship. The minister should be proficient in selecting hymns for their religious thought and poetic excellence, but should rely upon the choir director to use tunes that accord with principles they have agreed upon together. Both choir director and congregation will respect the minister's choices more readily if they feel he or she knows what is appropriate. Anyone is a traitor to the office and its inherent responsibilities if the whole matter is dismissed by saying, "I don't know anything about music" or "Sing anything, I'm tone deaf." It is patently true that "the minister . . . is probably the most important person to church music, for its level cannot rise higher than his [her] estimation of its importance in the life of the church."[3]

(2) Both minister and choir director should equip themselves with an adequate knowledge of the place of music in the history of the Reformed tradition and find occasions on which they can share it with the congregation. On Reformation Sunday, for example, the people may be told how the Reformers gave the heritage of religious music back to the people or how the Wesleyan revival in England opened a new chapter in the ministry of sacred song. Furthermore, neither minister nor choir director should ever berate in public the musical tastes of sincere Christian folk who are living up to the only insights they have had.

(3) The minister should take every opportunity available to encourage the choir director and to indicate a competent interest in the program he or she is directing. These may include requests that the organ be kept in proper condition mechanically and that an adequate budget be available for

musical supplies, guest soloists, choir gowns, and proper library and storage facilities. The minister should assist the director by encouraging the congregation to sing the hymns, and if in pastoral visitation some person is discovered with competent vocal talent, the name should be passed on to the director as a prospective chorister; no minister, however, should invite persons on his or her own to join the choir. Good music in the church is also a part of the Christian education program and, therefore, any minister should be especially grateful when it is done harmoniously and well.

(4) The minister should not attend choir rehearsals unless invited on occasion to do so. Some times the minister may want the choir to do a special portion of the act of worship in a certain way and therefore his or her presence at the rehearsal is needed; however, the minister will ask the director for permission to come in and indicate approximately the time when it is convenient.

(5) The choir is not a *performing* unit in the worship of the Reformed tradition. These choristers are meant to lead, but to do so among the congregation and as part of it. Nevertheless their regularity and faithfulness should not be allowed to go unnoticed or taken for granted. The minister should recognize their efforts occasionally by a word of praise or commendation. Such a positive word when properly said will enhance the quality of what is done to the glory of God. On the other hand, such rituals as dedications of choirs are alien to the Presbyterian worship tradition and, in view of what *The Directory of Worship* specifies, should be forbidden.

Guest Preacher

The term "guest preacher" is in a sense an anomaly, because anyone who has been ordained to the office of the Holy Ministry should not be considered as a "guest" in any church where he or she proclaims the whole gospel of God. Yet we must face the fact that this term has become an accepted description in the vocabulary of the Reformed tradition.

Anyone who is a "guest preacher" for even a little time discovers very soon the advantages and disadvantages of this office. On the positive side one can witness with comparative ease and can be even sharply prophetic without fear of indictment by one's hearers. Visiting ministers are not responsible, moreover, for any attendance index and are far removed from all the routine machinery of which the formal hour of worship is both the inspiration and the product. Theirs is a dramatic crossing of the stage, of which the props are not their invention, nor is their future reputation dependent upon them.

On the negative side there are some less heartening features. Guest preachers, for example, are rarely able to sense the particular moral and spiritual claim the strange congregation is making upon them. Its particular needs, pains, and sorrows are unknown and therefore guest preachers must try desperately to prevent their witness from becoming coldly impersonal and stolidly routine. Moreover, a guest minister is usually regarded as a "filler" in the absence of one who is the regular shepherd of the flock, or may be expected to vindicate and justify some advance notice to the effect that "our distinguished guest, despite an exceedingly busy schedule, has kindly consented to come to be with us today."

What is the experience of persons who are frequently called on as guest preachers? Generally their lot is more happy than painful. This is so because the great majority of our regular Presbyterian ministers either consciously or unconsciously make an effort to help the guest preacher feel at home. There is, however, a small minority of ministers who overlook—quite unintentionally, I believe—those little courtesies and fringe responsibilities that make their guest feel at ease, and themselves remembered later with deep appreciation. The following suggestions may help in some small way to make the bond of common interchange more real and to facilitate the ministry of visiting preachers as they move in and out.

(1) At least a week in advance, the host minister should

send in writing to the guest preacher a memo indicating *time* and *place* of the service, and the best route by which to travel. Who has not driven in desperation along the nameless streets of a strange city for an eleven o'clock service which perchance for the summer season has been advanced without warning to ten?

(2) Include among the directions a copy of the church bulletin or calendar with exact instructions regarding every important move to be made in conducting the various acts in the hour of worship. The rubrics are frequently very vague in some forms of Presbyterian worship.

(3) If the service is to commemorate or to be in recognition of a special event, the guest preacher should be informed of the type of service he or she is expected to lead and the length of time to speak, and given any other suggestions that may assist in his or her preparation. It can be exceedingly disconcerting to a guest preacher, who has a special twenty-five-minute sermon in readiness, to be told at 10:45 A.M. that a baptism, reception of new members, and the dedication of a memorial plaque are also included in the service of the day!

(4) If the service includes Holy Communion, it is extremely important that express directions be given beforehand. Better still, the elders should meet early with the guest preacher for an opportunity to brief one another in every action around the Table and thereby to forestall clumsiness and to prevent any unnecessary blunders.

(5) An elder should be selected to meet the guest preacher at the church entrance and show him or her to the vestry. The same elder should bring the organist along later so that final details may be clearly arranged.

(6) Finances are sometimes an embarrassing matter in the program of the Kingdom, but even in God's work, the laborer is worthy of his hire. No guest preacher, however, ought to be asked to set a fee, nor should expenses be discussed openly in the vestibule, and certainly an honorarium should not be presented with an ostentatious flourish.

(7) If a ministerial friend is invited to preach at an ordination or installation, and he or she is a member of the same presbytery, as a presbyter one should do it gladly and as a service to the presbytery and not expect any remuneration. If, however, one has to travel several hundred miles, there should be reimbursement at least for expenses.

(8) A few days after his or her visit, it is a gracious gesture to send a short letter of appreciation to the guest preacher.

Vestments

Any uniformity in clerical dress among Presbyterian ministers has never been realized, particularly in America. Presently, however, there appears to be a growing recognition of its value and propriety, and as a result many of the old arguments against a vested clergy are no longer advocated. Puritan opposition to anything that bore resemblance to Rome, and the curious American procedure of democratizing through similarity of dress have done much to make it necessary for the Protestant minister always to appear as "one of the boys." The old contention that clerical dress separates clergy and laity or minister and people has actually no foundation in experience and with rare exceptions has been proved to be sheer nonsense. The Presbyterian minister who dresses according to the dignity and propriety of the office is far more likely to have people turn to him or her for counsel than to the person who indulges in professional anonymity by means of a sports jacket, blue denims, and/or Adidas. A minister may be clubbish on the golf course or at the ball park where everyone is healthy and happy and were religion appears to have little place among life's essentials, but when the world tumbles in for one of the parishioners and the future is a grim step into the dark, the sporty minister may be bypassed by those who need sorely the comfort the church can give.

This is not to imply for one moment that clothes make the person. There is an opinion widely held, however, that the minister's attire should be a constant reminder that the clergy cannot be just other people among the crowd, but must be God's people among the people of the world. It is curious to note, moreover, the inconsistency in much of the clerical dress among Presbyterians. Many ministers who repudiate a clerical collar and the rabat vest and bands which, they claim, have no ecclesiastical meaning, will wear an academic hood which is not and never has been symbolic of anything related to the ministerial office. Indeed, the academic hood possesses less traditional warrant than those other articles of dress they have spurned. In view of this odd variety of usages, is it not time to invite a review of clerical dress in order to encourage the recognition of what is at least meaningful in a churchly sense and to suggest caution with what might be interpreted as articles of display? George Hedley's comment is appropriate here: "The church is not a university, and the minister in its services should wear not professorial but *churchly* garments. When he does so he will better reflect his true office, and incidentally he will be much easier to look at."[4]

Clerical dress generally is of secular origin. Only by association with the ministerial office has it taken on symbolic meaning. Indeed, clerical dress at many stages of history, chiefly on account of the conservatism of the church, was merely the common style of a previous generation. For example, the frock coat or "Prince Albert," which became the trademark of some clergy in this century, was merely the street clothes of the generation before. The purpose behind all clerical garments is to efface personal characteristics and to enhance the dignity of the office. A clerical collar never engenders adulation for the person, but it does symbolize the intention of a group to serve. To quote Dr. Hedley again, "With the collar he does become a visible, living reminder that some men have given themselves wholly to God, and that they are not ashamed of their high calling in Christ Jesus."[5]

The most familiar articles of dress for Presbyterian ministers both through custom and tradition include the Genevan gown, cassock, collar and bands, and stole. These efface idiosyncrasies of dress and symbolize certain responsibilities of office.

Even prior to the Reformation the gown was in common use among the clergy.[6] There were, of course, the elaborate liturgical vestments of the Roman tradition, but two articles were of private clerical use: the cassock and the gown. The cassock, which was of full length and had an upright collar, could be worn on any ordinary occasion and was really the forerunner of the short clerical coat. The gown was worn by the clergy as they walked to and from the church building; also it was used generally by the preacher in the pulpit, while the celebrant at the altar might be clothed in more elaborate liturgical vestments. The Reformers, however, reacted to vestments according to individual temperaments. Zwingli ruled them out entirely. Luther wore the monk's habit during morning worship and a regular doctor's gown for the afternoon service, although more elaborate historic vestments were continued in many churches throughout Germany. The Thirty Years' War (1618–1648) wrought many changes, including a wave of indifference toward all vestments, and the rise of pietism and rationalism created a climate somewhat inimical to ceremonial and the wide array of symbolism it perpetuated.

The simple black gown survived, however, and its continued universal use is due not a little to precedents set in Geneva. As Luther Reed has remarked, "The modern universal use of the black gown by Lutheran clergymen in Geneva has come about rather as a result of Calvinistic influence than because of the earlier use of it in the pulpit by Luther."[7] Among Presbyterians today the Genevan styled gown is generally accepted as a uniform article of pulpit dress. Whether or not it should be black is a moot question. Scott F. Brenner complains of our unwarranted non-use of white in the vestments of those who minister in worship, and he makes a case in its favor that is highly plausible.[8] On the other hand, some others might establish a case for blue with equally strong arguments. None of us, moreover, can agree with Luther Reed's sweeping statement that "black gowns are oppressively suggestive of a Calvinistic conception of worship."[9] He is right, however, in urging the use of colors symbolic of "the joy of Christian service," but he would acknowledge undoubtedly that the responsibility of the person in the act of worship must never be deferred to the color or texture of the cloth.

The cassock was originally the "walking out" dress for all clergy. Among Reformed ministers it was shortened like a coat of black silk or a modification of the longer cassock of the Church of England. Its style and consistency of use have varied. For example, in 1610 King James VI of Scotland ordered all bishops and doctors of divinity to wear short cassocks. From 1630 onward in Britain clergy appear in gown, cassock, and bands. A portrait of Alexander Henderson, Moderator of the Glasgow General Assembly in 1638, shows him wearing all three articles of clerical attire. But no custom continued with any regularity before the middle of the nineteenth century. In 1870 a photograph of Norman MacLeod shows a cassock, but in 1872 when Dean Stanley of Westminster preached in St. Andrew's Parish Church, the minister said, "The Dean wore similar garments to those worn by Scot ministers—gown, bands, and hood." It would appear, in view of such intermittent use, that the cassock has never secured general acceptance among Presbyterian clergy either in America or abroad. Many find the cassock too heavy when included with a Genevan gown and therefore choose instead a rabat vest for physical comfort.

The bands are of medieval origin and have both ecclesiastical and legal significance. Today in the church they are regarded or interpreted as an indication that a person is ordained and particularly the minister of a recognized congregation. Their exact origin is obscure. Some say that they are a relic of the big Tudor collars of the sixteenth and seventeenth centuries; others claim they are related to the bibs bearded monks wore to keep their cassocks clean; and some others believe they are symbolic of the ancient tablets of the Law which the preacher teaches and the lawyer dispenses.[10] In

the Reformed churches in England and Scotland they appear
as early as 1566. The occupant of the pulpit in St. Giles on the
day of Jenny Geddes' incident (July 23, 1637) wore bands.
Their association has continued with various appeals to prec-
edent and tradition and, like the gown, their use has never
been the property of any one branch of the Reformed tradition. Nathaniel Micklem, for example, in *Congregationalism
and the Church Catholic,* said, "The Congregational minister
in his traditional and proper dress, cassock and gown and
bands, is not aping the Roman priesthood but is the very symbol of the Reformed religion."[11]

The stole has come into more general use from the mid-
nineteenth century to the present day. Chaplains in both
world wars have accentuated its significance. A search
through old prints, however, will indicate its early use by
John Knox and Andrew Melville. Portraits of moderators of
the Church of Scotland since 1890 indicate its growing use,
and indeed in the United Free Assembly in 1925 the moderator wore a stole. Stoles are usually ornamented, for example,
with a Chi Rho or a cross. The use of colored ones by Reformed churches on the European continent is increasing, especially since hoods do not form part of the universal clerical
costume. The stole is the most ancient and meaningful of all
articles of clerical dress because it is regarded as a symbol of
the yoke of service.

Bulletin

No minister should be happy or remain satisfied with a
drab, disorderly, and unattractive Sunday bulletin. In a day in
which sales corporations and business firms place in our
hands brochures and pamphlets of the finest caliber, should
the church distribute among its people only third-rate print-
ing and designing? It is true that most printed orders and pro-
grams are costly and that even the least expensive should
never be permitted to become an end in itself. Most churches,
however, can afford a better quality of materials than simply

what "gets by." No commercial company which takes the slightest degree of pride in its product would tolerate for a moment a brochure that features smudgy mimeographing, typographical errors, amateur copy setting, unsightly cover designs, and announcements marred by bad grammar or hurried composition. Is there any reason why these should be countenanced or overlooked in the church? Or, what is equally serious, can we afford to perpetuate the notion that in the church "anything will do"?

The following suggestions are given to encourage care and deliberate judgment in preparing the format of the weekly bulletin and thereby to create a better aid to worship and a respectable channel for conveying information regarding the work and witness of the congregation.

(1) The minister of even a small church with a limited budget should strive to have the best bulletin under the circumstances. Usually any professional art or show card designer will gladly give advice regarding balance, type, composition, and arrangement. In some cases the local printer is willing to assist the minister in exploring ways of having a good job done with a reasonable financial outlay.

(2) A meaningful order of worship is weakened if it is crowded into inadequate space or so closely set that there is no apparent thought for beauty of arrangement or balance or proper grouping.

(3) The cover of the bulletin is important. It should suggest worship and not the extent of the congregation's real estate. Pictures of the entire church "plant" that fill the whole cover of the bulletin are neither inspirational nor meaningful and should be omitted. When parishioners pick up the bulletin it should remind them primarily of the worship of God rather than call attention to a physical structure that may not excel as a model of architectural design. Possibly a soaring spire that fades out at its base, the name of the church in tasteful letters, a prayer or apt quotation about worship, should be ample materials for a cover design. Many congregations are using bulletin covers already prepared by their denomina-

tional headquarters or by companies whose designing and lithographing craft is of superior quality.[12] These excel in rich symbolism, modest coloring, and varied lines of design. Some religious bookstores distribute yearly subscriptions for weekly bulletin covers, but generally the quality of the art, coloring, and composition compares easily with that of the comic strips of the Sunday newspaper.

(4) The bulletin should contain only what enhances the worship and work of the church. The announcements should be blocked neatly for easy reading, written in concise English, and free from anything that suggests an inappropriate type of humor. All must be within the context of a religious aim and the propriety that is associated with it.

(5) There should be a section, preferably the back cover, where the names of the minister, the staff (if any), and the various board chairpersons may be listed. Once or twice a year the entire personnel of the various boards should be printed in order that the congregation may be informed. If it is traditional in a congregation to have the minister's academic degrees printed after his or her name, no one should criticize the custom. However, if it is done at all, and in cases where several ministers are on the staff, it should be inclusive. It is questionable whether the organist and choristers should be given a separate category, "The Ministry of Music." Music is certainly an aid to worship, but worship is something we offer to God. Music as a "ministry" suggests a therapeutic role which does only partial justice to those who wrote great sacred choral works as an act of adoration of their Creator. Moreover, there is no such order or designation in Presbyterian churches as "Minister of Music." Its use in our churches is entirely without any warrant from official documents or by the General Assembly.

(6) The term "Reverend" is generally misused by Presbyterian congregations. It is an adjective, not a title. It is not the same as "Dean", for example, and should be used only in talking *about* a minister and not *to* a minister. Strictly speaking it should be used with the *whole* name and not with the

surname only. The proper form is "The Reverend John Smith," or "The Reverend Joan Sheppard." To use the term "Rev. Smith" or "Rev. Sheppard" either verbally or in print is as bad as saying to a governor, "Good morning, Honorable."

Worship Setting

Much is being said and written these days about church architecture, and certainly the ecclesiastical buildings in the newer areas of American "suburbia" are indicative of a desire to express multiple tastes, experiments, and ideals. Someone has said that churches should be built from the inside out. This means that what is done in the act of worship, when God's Word and God's people meet in the worship encounter, should determine the arrangement of the interior furnishings and the outward shape of the building. This emphasizes the importance of designing meaningfully the worship center where things are done. This center is not, however, any one special place within the building, such as a shrine; it is commensurate with the dimensions of the room because the whole congregation is involved. As Gilbert Cope has said, "Church buildings ... should not be thought of as existing in their own right, but basically as serviceable shelters for a group of people liturgically in action."[13] This action is important and determinative, and nothing should slight its integrity or impede its work lest it be merely a truncated expression of what, according to God's purpose, it should be. The liturgy, we must understand, is a creative thing in which living people are involved, and its outward character and inner cohesion become real to the degree that the Christian community realizes its common life in Jesus Christ.

In view of these ideas it is important that the best thinking be given to structural planning both by congregational committees and by the professional architect. Often disastrous and costly bungling occurs because the church's planning committee is so uninformed about the meaning of its act of worship and the varied functions of its mission in the community that it provides no assistance to the architects, especially when they ask some very sensible questions. Often they are left in what Harold E. Wagoner has called "the middle of a big Presbyterian nowhere." On the other hand, occasionally some architects are more interested in creating monuments to themselves or their experimental prowess than to the glory of God. Much time is saved and embarrassment avoided if there is "careful and thoughtful study by the individual church of its own beliefs, its own attitudes and expressions of worship, its own traditions as well as those of the parent communion, *before* the architect ever comes on the scene."[14] Indeed a good beginning can always be made if the committee is prepared to answer adequately the architects' initial question, "What do you believe about God?"

Fortunately in the matter of architecture certain illusions are fading gradually and Presbyterian worship stands to benefit as a result. Gothic is no longer seen as a sacrosanct form of ecclesiastical architecture or as the norm for all Christian traditions. The chancel, which was originally a special place for the monks in the medieval church and which became obsolete after the Reformation, experienced in America a period of revival in this century as a rostrum for performing choirs, but the contemporary redefinition of the role of the choir in Reformed worship has decided in favor of its location elsewhere. Actually there is no such thing as an architectural tradition for Presbyterian churches, but in the early stages of planning three factors should be kept in mind: function, doctrine, and sentiment.

(1) Function: What is the church building for? It is primarily to house a congregation for the worship of God, especially the hearing of his Word, and the celebration of the sacraments. It must be planned, therefore, so everyone can hear and see and the officiating clergy can perform their functions with ease. Each action that is traditionally carried out and each group involved, such as choirs, elders, deacons, and ushers, must be taken into account and the freedom and efficiency of its participation assured.

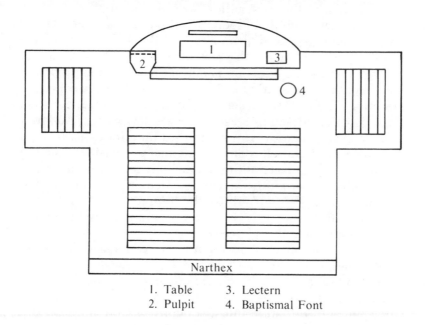

1. Table   3. Lectern
2. Pulpit   4. Baptismal Font

(2) Doctrine: The character of the setting with a Presbyterian church must reflect the central emphasis of the act of worship: the proclamation of the Word of God and the congregation's response to it. One of the better designs is an oblong building with broad transepts and a shallow semicircular apse. The long, narrow nave is never conducive either to hearing or to seeing. A broad nave with shallow transepts and rounded apse forms a closely knit unit and integrated entity. The communion table would stand in the center of the apse with a simple bench behind it and with pulpit and lectern on either side. Table, pulpit, and lectern would form a harmonious group: the lectern with the open Bible representing the Word read; the pulpit, the exposition of the Word; and the table, the Word in action. These are not separated entities—as critics of this setting argue—but are facets of one act: the

proclamation of the Word. Provision would be made for locating the choir in the west gallery over the narthex.

A modern example of lectern and pulpit combined and of "the gathering-around principle" in the fellowship of the Lord's Table appears in the next diagram.

Perennially the question is raised regarding the proper location of the baptismal font. In an eassy on "Baptismal Architecture," J. G. Davies states that in Calvinistic churches "baptismal architecture . . . simply does not exist."[15] And from a backward glance over the centuries he informs us that "in the majority of churches of the Calvinist persuasion a shallow basin was used, placed either on the holy table, that the sacrament might be administered in the face of the congregation, or in a bracket attached to the pulpit."[16] In the *Église Réformée* in France it is still the custom for a bowl to be carried in for the baptismal occasion.

In Presbyterian churches in America generally a baptismal font is located on the congregational level, maybe at the right or left at the front and in the vicinity of either the chancel or platform steps. Anyone who sees the sacrament of Baptism as the symbol of initiation into the family of God is opposed to two extremes that have appeared through the centuries in the architectural handling or placing of the font. The separate baptistery Davies calls "an anachronism" because its small dimensions permit the attendance of only a fraction of the congregation. The silver bowl, kept in a cupboard between times, suggests a treatment of baptism as a "second-class sacrament." In both these extreme cases, the vital importance of baptism in the community of God's worshiping people is apt to appear somewhat discounted. No one can legislate, however, when the varied facilities of so many diverse buildings are involved, but if the two sacraments—Baptism and the Lord's Supper—are of equal significance, we should want the liturgical place to be so arranged that from the viewpoint of seeing and using, neither of these symbolic objects should be deprived of its proper eminence.

(3) Sentiment: No church can be said to be "worshipful"

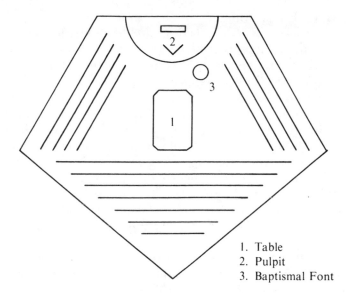

1. Table
2. Pulpit
3. Baptismal Font

unless it creates an atmosphere of reverence and peace. Simplicity is more likely than anything else to evoke a sense of the majesty of the Unseen. The close proximity of the people in keeping with the gathering-around principle makes them more truly participants. Nothing should interfere with or "obscure the fact that here God meets his people in order to give himself to them in a reconciling communion."[17] This means, as John Stewart Detlie put it, that "devotion is not something to be poured in by ritual; it must be mixed in the very essence of the mortar between its stones . . . Religious buildings must be built from the inside out, and in this sense *inside* means the spirit."[18]

Ushers

In many Presbyterian churches the responsibility for ushering at the regular services of worship is taken fully by the Board of Deacons. In some others there is a Board of Ushers which may have some deacons among its members or a deacon as its chairperson, but which does not assume the over-all duties for which a deacon is ordained and installed.

The following proprieties ought to be kept in mind by any group whose responsibility it is to assure order and decorum in the worship of the sanctuary:

(1) Ushers should be on hand in ample time before the stated hour of worship in order to be able to check miscellaneous items such as ventilation, lights, hymnbooks, the supply of bulletins, location of collection plates, and acousticon or hearing aid mechanisms.

(2) An usher should be neatly dressed, carefully groomed, and distinguishable by some identifying mark such as a boutonniere. In some large churches the formal attire of the ushers lends poise and dignity to the ushers' activity, which casual clothes could not do.

(3) An usher should not be required to serve every Sunday of the year. The number of available persons ought to be sufficiently large so that they may serve on teams under a chairperson or captain and on a monthly or quarterly schedule.

(4) Ushers should have a natural approach in handling the worshipers and should be careful to avoid cold affectation at one extreme or irksome unctuousness at the other. A head usher should be stationed in the narthex to direct people toward the various aisles in an attempt to assure uniformity of numbers in the seating areas. Where there are several entrances or when the influx becomes too great at 10:55 A.M. for one person to handle, assistants should be available. Each aisle needs two persons: one to hold people near the entrance while the other is escorting worshipers to their pew.

(5) Ushers should control the seating of latecomers and bring them down the aisles only at the designated points in the order of worship. In large churches there should be an understanding that the organist will improvise briefly until all are seated. Latecomers should not be permitted to overcrowd

convenient pews to the discomfort of those who arrived on time.

(6) An usher should inquire if worshipers would prefer to sit near the front or toward the center of the sanctuary. The usher may walk before them and stand beside the pew just ahead, passing a bulletin to them as they enter, and then returning to his or her post. If the usher should meet others moving down the aisle unescorted, he or she may ask if they would like to have assistance. People should be persuaded tactfully to move in to the center of each pew in order to provide easy access to others who may arrive later.

(7) Since most ushering is done during the organ prelude, ushers should do their work quietly and efficiently; there should be no noisy conversation or loud pleasantries exchanged within the sanctuary.

(8) It is an intolerable practice in many churches for ushers to go out for a smoke during a lull in their duties. Generally a service of worship is one hour's duration. Persons who cannot refrain from smoking during this period should reconsider their ability to serve. Moreover, it is equally undesirable for the official deacons of the congregation to use the period during the sermon as a time to sort out the offerings and count the money. A well-trained board of ushers will be seated in their own places at the ends of pews during the sermon and retire to their posts only at the close of the benediction. Some will be designated at this point to open all exits in order to expedite the emptying of the sanctuary, especially if another service follows within half an hour.

(9) The manner of receiving the offerings of the people will depend largely upon the physical design or layout of the seats in the sanctuary. Nevertheless, the way in which the ushers collect the offerings can contribute in no small way to maintaining a worshipful atmosphere and to giving a sense of meaning to an act which many people consider to be merely an interruption.

(10) It is useful for the minister to have some permanent record of Sunday attendance. Each usher can be responsible

for recording his or her own section. The head usher will keep the totals and record them along with any other useful information such as weather conditions, guest minister, or seasonal epidemics that affect attendance.

(11) Ushers should agree upon procedures if and when there is a case of fire, of sudden illness, or of some other imaginable calamity. They should note carefully where a physician may be seated if in any eventuality his or her assistance is required.

(12) Proper consideration must be given by all churches to local or state safety regulations regarding seating, especially on the occasion of an overflow congregation. In some localities, chairs either in the aisles or narthex are prohibited and all exits must be visibly marked.

LITERATURE FOR CHURCH ARCHITECTURE

Bruggink, D. J., and Droppers, C. H. *Christ and Architecture.* Grand Rapids: W. B. Eerdmans, 1963.

Christ-Janer, A., and Foley, M. *Modern Church Architecture.* New York: McGraw-Hill Book Co., 1962.

Davies, J. G. *The Architectural Setting of Baptism.* London: Barrie & Rockliff, 1962.

Drummond, A. L. *The Church Architecture of Protestantism.* Edinburgh: T. & T. Clark, 1934.

Fiddes, Victor. *The Architectural Requirements of Protestant Worship.* Toronto: The Ryerson Press, 1961.

Hammond, Peter (ed.). *Towards a Church Architecture.* London: Architectural Press, 1962.

Sovik, E.A. *Architecture for Worship.* Minneapolis: Augsburg Publishing House, 1973.

White, James F. *Protestant Worship and Church Architecture.* New York: Oxford, 1964.

9

The Service
of Ordination

In *The Form of Government* (United Presbyterian Church, U.S.A., Chap. XIX), two statements describe and summarize what the church specifies as its requirements to be fulfilled by each candidate for ordination to the exercise of his or her ministry.

Section 1: When a candidate for the ministry, having been under the care of a presbytery for at least one year and having received a bachelor's degree from a regionally accredited college or university, has completed his or her prescribed course of study in a recognized United Presbyterian Theological Seminary, or has offered an educational equivalent previously approved by presbytery and now judged satisfactory by it, and has satisfactorily completed the trials for ordination set forth in Section 2 (Chap. XIX), and has received a call acceptable to him or her and to presbytery, the presbytery shall take steps for his or her ordination. (This report on the candidate will include also the regular transcript from the Presbyteries' Cooperative Committee on Examinations for Ministerial Candidates.)

Section 5: An appearance by the candidate before the responsible committee of presbytery which shall satisfy itself as to the candidate's readiness in all aspects for ordination to the professional ministry. The committee's inquiry shall include but not be limited to the following: (a) discussion with the candidate of the results of the trials for ordination thus far; (b) the candidate's plans for continuing study and growth; (c) the acceptability of the candidate's views within the confessional standards of the Church; (d) the candidate's understanding of the import of the vows required for ordination; and (e) the candidate's commitment to the professional ministry within the discipline of The United Presbyterian Church in the United States of America.[1]

These statements set forth clearly the levels of achievement in instruction and theological understanding the church requires of each candidate at this stage in the process of preparing for and seeking ordination to, what *The Book of Common Worship* calls, "The office of the Holy Ministry." Unfortunately, however, few facilities and opportunities are provided generally for candidates to discover satisfactory answers to certain other questions which arise inevitably and with regularity whenever they contemplate this great step which, vocationally and devotionally, each of them is about to take. These questions lie more deeply than a simple, "What must I *do* as a Presbyterian to qualify for ordination?" They belong more properly to one's state of *being* and involve: (i) what are the origins and principles of ministry? (ii) what difference does ordination make? (iii) what is one's vocational deportment within the ministerial office *vis-à-vis* the church?

I

Origins and Principles of Ministry

One of the most comprehensive essays on the nature of the Christian ministry from biblical and historical perspectives is "The Christian Ministry" by J.B. Lightfoot.[2] Although written a century ago, no candidate for ordination can afford to forego some acquaintance with this comprehensive and scholarly treatise.

It is not our purpose here to claim credibility for any one system of ministry (i.e., hierarchical or free) as being the intention or design of Christ. Plausible arguments in abundance can be wrenched from any number of scriptural proof texts, and certainly, from the historical perspective, the latter part of the first century and much of the second are not helpful. Indeed Manson points out that "the episcopate, as it existed at Philippi and Corinth, and quite probably at Rome, in the first century, is indistinguishable from the presbyterate."[3] Moreover, currently in the multiple varieties of Christian denominationalism, to commit oneself to a particular brand is tantamount to accepting automatically its form of ministry anyway. Therefore, in our contemporary state of things in which institutions as such are evaluated more readily by means and not by ends, maybe greater credibility for the nature of ministry is to be found more properly among those characteristics which marked the exercise of ministry in the outreach of the early church.

Whenever the Christian ministry is mentioned, certain terms or specifics come readily to the mind of anyone familiar with the New Testament: call, sent, herald, servant, witness, care of souls, and so forth. These concepts do not occur in any ordered sequence in Scripture, but any unified perspective on ministry delineates a certain pattern of operation and fulfillment. Basic to any description of the Christian ministry is a sense of *call*, followed by direction and outward reach suggested by the word *sent*. However, no one is ever called or sent without a definite purpose. The Christian minister is a *herald* who is sent to *proclaim* that in God's scheme of things something happened, something has been done for us, and its benefits are such that he or she is moved to *witness* to it. Some people in every community will hear and accept this message gladly; others will need careful handling and tending and for this reason the minister must exercise effectively the *care of souls*.

It ought not to be implied, however, that a call to the ministry must be attested to by the candidate in terms of a specific day or hour when seemingly the lightning struck; a call means that, as John Line put it, "the ministry is first not of man but of God and of the will of Christ . . . Bereft of this, the ministry is an anomaly: as a bare human career or employment the most pedestrian and purposeless of all."[4] Every minister is where he or she is "through the decision of God."[5] "You did not choose me, but I chose you" (John 15:16). The call and the sense of being sent, moreover, imply a commission. In Scripture this is known by the Hebrew concept of *shaliach* in which there is a close identity between the caller and the called or, as Line wrote, "The sent is one with the sender."[6] "He who receives you receives me" (Matt. 10:40; John 13:20). This lifts the minister happily above the plane of being merely a practitioner. Prior to being called, being sent, and being a herald is the Word which is foundational. Every minister must reckon initially with the claim of that Word and as God's servant he or she accepts the great commission that the Gospel be preached to all nations (Mark 13:10; 16:15; Matt. 28:19). R.W. Dale once said, "Jesus did not come to preach a Gospel; he came that there might be a Gospel to preach." For the minister, the Gospel is a "given" and he or she is the medium the Holy Spirit chooses to witness to its redemptive efficacy before the world (Acts 1:8).

II

The Difference Ordination Makes

Generally in the Reformed tradition a tenet widely held and frequently misunderstood is "the priesthood of all believers." Many Protestants consider this concept to mean, "Everyone of us can be his or her own priest." This understanding is not only faulty but at variance with the New Testament and what the Reformers themselves had in mind. It does not mean that "each of us is his or her own priest," but the very opposite: "Each of us is priest to every other person." Hence it is a communal and not an individual concept; moreover, it emphasizes the necessity and indispensability of Christian community.

This clarification, however, leads to another problem: the dichotomy between "clergy" and "laity." It is a problem because it is a distinction made within the boundaries of the priesthood of all believers. Both terms appear in the New Testament, but they are used with reference to the same persons—the community of God's people.[7] They had a commonality with reference to church members just as *diakonia* had for "ministry" (every Christian was a servant, a minister). This is why Hendrik Kraemer used the phrase, "the Church is ministry."[8] However, the Reformers were realists also and therefore they set apart certain persons to exercise a more specialized form of ministry; these were ordained (i.e., "set apart") to preach the Word of God and to administer the sacraments. Without this format or system there would be chaos in the church; as John Mackay intimated, there would be "ardor without order."

The act of setting certain persons apart for service in the Church can be accepted and interpreted rightfully within the Reformed tradition as "a distinction without a difference." It lies, first of all, in the matter of function. The essence of ministry may not be higher qualitatively in the person of the clergy than any one of the laity, but the exercise of ministry in the case of the former requires fuller preparation in order to effect through intellectual and spiritual gifts and competence the salvation of the parish community.[9] But the matter does not end there, for, as Charles Hodge stated, "the ministry is an office, and not merely a work."[10]

This distinction lies more properly, therefore, in the matter of office, not in a hierarchical sense, but in terms of vocational wholeness. To quote Hodge further:

> An office is a station to which the incumbent must be appointed, which implies certain prerogatives, which it is the duty of those concerned to recognize and submit to. A work, on the other hand, is something which any man who has the ability may undertake . . . not every one who has the qualifications for the work of the ministry . . . can assume the office of the ministry. He must be regularly appointed.[11]

And Calvin declared that "authority and dignity are inherent in the office itself, or better still, in the Word of God, to serve which the person concerned is called."[12]

In the act of ordination, function and office come together when (i) through the prayers of intercession of the church and the endorsement of the candidate's suitability and proficiency by the church through its representatives, the attention of the community of God's people is focused upon the chosen person; (ii) through an appeal for the descent and continued presence of the Holy Spirit ('ἐπικαλέω) and by the laying on of the hands of presbytery, the church makes explicit what was implicit in and through the original act of God; and (iii) the inner submission and commitment of the candidate to the claim and blessing of the Holy Spirit allows the latter to determine the form of and become operative in the function of ministry. Whenever an ordination of a candidate takes place, the action is not intended to focus upon function or status, but in the drama of the rite the essential character of the office is portrayed and the church sees in this action the re-presentation of its own ministry.[13] In Acts 1:8 we read, "But you shall receive power when the Holy Spirit has come upon you; and you shall be my witnesses in Jerusalem and in all Judea and Samaria and to the end of the earth."

The cruciality of this act is suggested by Harry G. Goodykoontz when he wrote, "There is no greater moment in the life of a minister than the hour when he is ordained. It is quite likely the deepest spiritual experience of his life. Outwardly he is the same person, but inwardly the Holy Spirit is at work, as he becomes a minister of Word and Sacrament."[14] The impressiveness of this moment, moreover, in the experience of the candidate is accentuated and made more real by those denominations which retain fortunately in their rite of ordination the sequence when the Moderator (after the ordination prayer, the laying on of hands, and the candidate rises) presents him or her with a Bible and *The Book of Common Worship* (or whatever Service Book it may be) and says:

> "Take thou authority to preach the Word of God and to minister the holy Sacraments in the congregation."

No one hearing and taking this mandate seriously can fail to recognize it as anything other than a great watershed in his or her life; everything is cast now into a before and after. Both function and office are joined as the outer and inner facets of a ministry in which "the work being of God must be done in the power of God and directed by him."[15]

III

The Ministerial Office Within the Church

We have seen, then, that the making of a minister is an act of God. "Ordination," writes John M. Barkley, "is an act of God through presbyters within the people of God." In Scotland they spoke of "a double call: 'called of God and duly elected by men.' The 'call' of the people was seen as confirming the inward 'call' of God. The Holy Spirit works not only in the candidate, but also in the electors."[16] Or, as John Line comments, "the Spirit chooses and consecrates a human medium for His own operation."[17] The church's certification of this action will depend, however, upon (i) the genuineness of the candidate's response to his or her call; (ii) the capability of the candidate to exercise a fruitful ministry; and (iii) the extent to which "the will of the ordinand and the will of the Church are united in an act of dedication to the service of God and man."[18] This latter responsibility is more likely to be fulfilled if the minister's long range sense of vocation is understood as his or her being "a servant of the Word and of the Church begotten of the Word."[19] As ministers of the Word they preach, teach, celebrate the sacraments, and exercise the care of souls. Their authority for doing all these things is not something added; it is the authority of the Word from which the individual minister received first his or her call and in responding to it, accepted it as a gift and with it he or she was empowered by the Spirit. (Luke 9:1, 2). And it is within the church all this occurs and continues.

The entire church with its ministry is sent into the world. We must think of the church as being always "in mission." The ordained ministry whom God has called and the church has set apart to a role of representativeness within the company of God's people must safeguard and bring to fruition the nature and mission of the church in every generation. As P.T. Forsyth said to a company of ministers and students at Yale University over a half-century ago, "[You are] so to preach to the Church from the Gospel so that with the Church [you] may preach the Gospel to the world."[20] Ordination, moreover, takes place within the context of an act of worship and is associated inseparably with the church's unceasing celebration of what God has done for us in Jesus Christ and what he continues to do in and through its ministry. The new ordinand owes to the church a responsibility to lead a life of witness, reconciliation, and service and to be a medium through which the Apostolic faith is perpetuated and transmitted; on the other hand, the church owes the new ordinand a responsibility never to lose a sense of its own part as a world-wide organism in the redemptive ministry of the living Christ. An ordination, then, is an occasion for thanksgiving, not only for the fact of God's deed of love, but also because through the church and its ministry love's redeeming act is going on. God has called another leader and enabler, a herald and a servant, and the candidate's decisive response and the church's acceptance and recognition of it, are evidences of his Grace in action. A service of ordination is an appropriate time to praise God and sing: "Holy, holy, holy, Lord God of hosts, heaven and earth are full of thy glory; Glory be to thee, O Lord most high!"

Ordination Service

Services of special significance are frequent in many churches, yet there is never any reason for their not being meaningfully arranged and tastefully conducted. Two services of unusual importance to every minister are (1) ordination and (2) the installation that occurs whenever a minister begins a new pastorate. Since these services are under the direction of the presbytery with divers clergy and laypersons involved, not infrequently they are poorly conducted and interminably long, and present so many voices taking diminutive parts that the total impression is fragmentary. These occasions are the high and memorable experiences of any person's ministry and no one should permit their being badly handled by inept presbyters or executed in a hurried manner.

In the case of ordination, candidates will select as the place either their home church or the church to which they have been called. In the event of the latter choice the service will be in all likelihood a combined ordination and installation. The order of service will be set by the candidate and both order and participants who are invited must be approved by the presbytery. If invitations are sent out and a special bulletin printed, the candidate should work out these details with the session of the church, since some extra expense is involved.

The ordination service (and maybe installation) will be conducted by the moderator or vice-moderator, except in cases where a layperson is serving and a fellow presbyter has been appointed from among themselves; generally, however, the preacher is a close friend of the ordinand—a college or seminary professor, a former minister, or some clergy who has figured prominently in one's religious pilgrimage. Two charges are given: one to the ordinand; the other, if there is an installation also, to the congregation. The ordination prayer is offered by the moderator of presbytery; only in special cases, such as when a layperson is serving as moderator, is it done by anyone else.

The order of worship may be as follows:

Prelude
Call to Worship
Hymn of Praise
Prayer of Adoration
Prayer of Confession
Assurance of Pardon
Lesson(s)
Anthem
Sermon
Hymn
Service of Ordination
    The Constitutional Questions (printed in full in bulletin)
    The Prayer of Ordination
    The Laying on of Hands
    The Declaration

Charge to Ordinand (6-8 minutes)
Solo or Anthem
Charge to Congregation (6-8 minutes)
Hymn
Benediction by Ordinand
Postlude

Some orders have a brief prayer of intercession after the lessons; if so, it should focus upon the work and mission of the church of Christ and not be a preview of matters appropriate for the ordination prayer.

Appropriate Lessons for this service are:

Old Testament	New Testament (Gospels)
Isaiah 6:1–8	Matthew 16:13–20; 24–28
Isaiah 40:1–11; 27–31	Luke 9:1–6; 18–26
Isaiah 61:1–4	John 10:1–16
Jeremiah 1:4–12; 17–19	John 12:20–36
Ezekiel 37:1–10	John 15:1–17
	John 21:15-19

New Testament (Epistles)

Romans 12:1–13	Ephesians 4:1–16
1 Corinthians 3:9–23	Philippians 2:1–10
1 Corinthians 12:27—13:1–13	2 Timothy 2:1–15
2 Corinthians 4:1–12	2 Timothy 4:1–5

For hymn selections (other than the opening hymn):

"O Spirit of the Living God" (James Montgomery)
"Christ Is Made the Sure Foundation" (Latin, c. 7th century, Trans. John Mason Neale)
"I Love Thy Kingdom, Lord" (Timothy Dwight)
"Come, Holy Ghost, Our Souls Inspire" (Latin, c. 9th century, Trans. John Cosin)
"Holy Spirit, Truth Divine"(Samuel Longfellow)
"Spirit of God, Descend upon My Heart" (George Croly)
"O Thou Who Camest from Above" (Charles Wesley)
"Lord, Speak to Me" (Frances R. Havergal)
"I'm Not Ashamed to Own My Lord" (Isaac Watts)
"God of the Prophets" (Denis Wortman)
"The Church's One Foundation" (Samuel J. Stone)

LITERATURE FOR ORDINATION

Hodge, Charles. *What Is Presbyterianism?* Philadelphia: Presbyterian Board of Publication, 1855.

Goodykoontz, H.G. *The Minister in the Reformed Tradition.* Richmond: John Knox Press, 1963.

Line, John. *The Doctrine of the Christian Ministry.* Toronto: The Ryerson Press, 1959.

Manson, T.W. *The Church's Ministry.* Philadelphia: The Westminster Press, 1948.

Paul, R.S. *Ministry.* Grand Rapids: Wm. B. Eerdmans, 1965.

Mudge, L.S. & Cochrane, A.C. *Model for Ministry.* Report of Special Committee on the Theology of the Call. General Assembly of the United Presbyterian Church, U.S.A., 1970.

ORDINATION RITES

The Book of Common Worship. The Presbyterian Church in the U.S.A., 1946 edition.

The Book of Common Order. The Presbyterian Church in Canada, pp. 348–361, 1964 edition.

10
Two Sermons
on Worship

1. The Rediscovery of Praise*

*"Praise ye the LORD. Praise God in his sanctuary. . . .
Let everything that hath breath, praise ye the LORD!"*
Psalm 150:1 & 6 (K.J.V.)

Once Harry Emerson Fosdick observed that there were
four reasons why some people came to church—and all four of
them, he indicated, were wrong. There are those who come
because they think it is the decent, customary thing to do in
the average American community on Sunday morning. There
are those who come because they are fans of popular preachers, just as some others are devotees of certain TV or
Hollywood stars. Then there are those who come because
they think the church is a good thing; it helps one's reputation; and after all, religion does go hand in hand with social
respectability. And finally, there are those who come because
they think of worship as being something of a glorified aspirin
tablet which is bound to guarantee them peace of mind.

If any of these were the basic reason for attending worship, then from the Christian perspective it would not be
worthwhile to come at all. Here Fosdick was reminding us
that we do not come to church primarily to feel better, or to be
inspired, or even to be informed, although certainly these can
and ought to be the by-products of any genuine act of worship. We come for one particular and peculiar purpose—un-

---

*Preached in the Chapel of Princeton University.

like any other organization upon this earth; we come
according to the tradition of the Old and New Testaments: *we
come to praise God.* This is why throughout the whole of
Christendom on every Sunday morning, in churches small
and great, in Gothic cathedrals and in tiny meeting houses,
there rise from joyful men and women the full, rich notes of
the tune *Old Hundredth* as they sing:

> Praise God from whom all blessings flow;
> Praise him, all creatures here below;
> Praise him above, ye heavenly host:
> Praise Father, Son, and Holy Ghost.

By now I imagine, someone in this congregation is fight-
ing back. Come to church to praise God? "Why," I hear you
say, "that's a new one." Indeed someone else joins in and
adds, "In my ordering of priorities, praise is pretty far down
the list." Why? Because the word "praise" confuses us: at one
moment we reach for it; at the next it embarrasses us and we
shrink from it. And the reason is that we are inclined to
understand praise only in its secular sense and rarely in its
religious sense. In its secular sense today it is almost "a six-
letter" word. Unfortunately when we use it in a religious context we tend merely to transfer it laterally and to bring its secular meaning with it. This is why, for the average person,
praise would be an unlikely reason for coming to church.

Take praise, for instance in its secular sense. Usually it has
overtones which are suspect or it brings along with it a bad
connotation. It is placed in the same bracket with the sirens of
Greek mythology who lured their victims to their own de-
struction. An old maxim reads, "He who loves praise, loves
temptation." William Cowper, the eighteenth century poet,
said, "The thirst for praise is the substitute for genius, sense,
and wit." And John Keble, the English divine, referred to
praise as "a blind guide with a siren's voice." Indeed, in
everyday dialogue, praise seems to be heir to treacherous un-
dercurrents; it raises questions about the one who freely
gives it and it can malign the one who really delights in re-

ceiving it. Hence praise has been dogged by such parentheses as these: "Beware of Greeks bearing gifts." "Avoid the [person] with an axe to grind." And who among us, at some time or another, has not suffered the fate of "being damned with faint praise." Guilt by association has struck a mortal blow against one of the great words of our religious tradition and with it the element of praise has been dropped from so much of our Christian worship.

But such was never the case with the Old and New Testaments. Every great act of faith in the Scriptures is accompanied and enlivened by an outburst of praise. The Book of Psalms, the hymnbook of the Hebrew people, pulses consistently with the rhythmic cadences of *Praise Ye the Lord!* And in the New Testament, whenever little companies of redeemed men and women met, we read, "The whole multitude of the disciples began to rejoice and praise God for all the mighty works that they had seen" (Luke 19:37). Or, "they returned to Jerusalem with great joy, and were continually in the temple praising and blessing God" (Luke 24:53). Or, it was said of the lame man whom Peter healed at the Gate Beautiful that "he ... entered the temple with them, walking and leaping and praising God" (Acts 3:8). For these people, worship would not be worship at all without the element of praise. And their praises were spontaneous outbursts of human gratitude for the wonderful works of the living God in and through their own experience.

Now, let us come to ourselves. My thesis here today is this: the reason so much of our worship is dull, meaningless, and unfruitful to people inside and outside the church is simply because we have lost the indispensable note of praise. Praise can be the index to the genuineness of our worship, for if we cannot praise or if our praise is thin and sluggish, our worship has in all probability no underpinning, no objective, or no claim to viability in this topsy-turvy world. The Psalmist sang, "Praise ye the Lord. Praise God in the sanctuary. Let everything that hath breath praise the Lord." His call gives us our topic: the rediscovery of praise. It is not too much to say that the rediscovery of praise will mean not only the restoration of brightness and verve to our churches. It can give new vitality to every component and activity of our common faith. For as James S. Stewart of Edinburgh said, "Whenever you get real religion, you can be sure of this: the dominant note will be praise."

I

In view of what we have seen, the first observation I would like to make is: *the rediscovery of praise will come with the wholeness of our belief.*

Not long ago I attended a service of worship which began with the leader asking everyone to stand and shake hands with his or her neighbor and sing a sprightly jingle by Avery and Marsh. It reminded me of the opening of the program of a service club when everyone joins in

> The more we are together,
> Together, together!
> The more we are together
> The happier we'll be!

Now, it was fun! But I have taken part in May-pole dances which had as much meaning. Why? Because it was merely a fellowship of fun. It was only a superficial attempt which did not fulfill those basic requirements that can produce the joy of real Christian fellowship. The Psalmist said, "Praise ye the Lord!" And he called his people to use trumpets, harps, and cymbals to augment their overture of praise. But when we read these psalms carefully and prayerfully we sense how these praises were in essence an upsurge of their whole life in response to who God was and what they knew him to be in every part of their daily experience.

One evening some months ago I attended a dinner with some twenty professors from a number of disciplines of the theological field. Afterwards our host, who is one of the keenest minds in the theological world today, asked us informally what we thought the direction of theological thinking would take in the next decade. Various individuals ventured answers; but, curiously enough, the eldest person in the group—an octogenarian—spoke up and predicted that the theological thinking of the next decade would be preoccupied likely with this question: "How does one experience God?" It is interesting to note that throughout the history of theological thinking in the western world, there have been periods when great minds have woven magnificent theories about the nature and being of God, but gradually and inevitably the pendulum swung to a renewed concern for personal religious experience, its possibilities, its reality, and its benefits. The human voice cries out eventually, "This is all very well. But where in my life does it take root?" This is the concluding note to the story of your belief and mine and when we realize it in depth, we cannot suppress our praise.

Herein, moreover, lies the difference between praise and thanksgiving. We *thank* God for all he gives us: our food, our clothing, our families, our health and so forth. But we *praise* God for *who* and *what he is*. Praise keeps us from thanking God merely for material handouts. Many people can call God their Creator and Provider, but few are able to come to terms with what the nature of his being should mean to them. To experience him is to know him in our own life: how he loves us; why he is concerned about us; and what is the best he intends for us. These are real items in the story of our individual Christian belief. You and I may wonder at some of the great theories which are formulated about the nature and being of God, but when we see the outworking of his will and purpose in human experience, our natural inclination is praise.

I remember when I was a lad a series of revival services was held in the village church. During that week a miracle occurred: the local drunk was converted. All through the years his saintly wife had borne in silence the sorrow and shame of his wretched reputation and their four strong sons had endured with quiet courage all the abuse and domestic wrangling in the home. But there came that Sunday morning when their father led in prayer in the village church. That mother had heard much through the years from the pulpit about God as Creator, Sustainer, and Sanctifier, but on that day she saw her faith come full circle and turning to a group of simple woman folk in the vestibule, she said with a strange radiance on her face, "Praise the Lord!"

II

There is a second observation: *The rediscovery of praise will come when we know the true meaning of worship.*

We said at the outset that we come to church to praise the Lord. This may startle some of us because it seems out of character for even the sincerest believer; and what is more, it runs counter to the traditional point of view. Most people will claim they go to church on Sunday to get inspiration to live the good life during the week or to "rev up" their spiritual motors to perform works of mercy and help. All this is quite worthy, but it has done much to damage the reputation of the church before the eyes of the outside world. People do not always come out of church eager and zealous for good works; very often they emerge more settled in their old complacencies. People do not always come out of church rearing to take up cudgels against the evils of the nation and society; very often they depart with all their inner prejudices reconfirmed. And this will continue to be the case unless and until all of us get back to an understanding of the meaning of praise in the New Testament.

The early Christians did not say to one another: let us put up a building on the town square where we can hold services on Sunday morning at eleven o'clock and thereby get the spiritual dynamic to carry us through the week. On the contrary: they were born again men and women who had already infiltrated their community, touching other lives here and there, witnessing to what the spirit of Christ had done in them, and turning lost creatures into real people saved by grace. Then on Sunday morning, the day associated with Christ's resurrection, they crowded into homes, halls, and olive groves and praised God for the miracles which had occurred. The church was not to them some sort of hot-box where people were stirred up by jingles and rhythms and which sent them out with blueprints for the economic re-ordering of the world. The worship of these people had an entirely different meaning. It consisted of the praises of people who, during the week, had seen the gospel—their gospel—working the wonders of salvation among their fellows: the wounded were healed; the blind were given their sight; the broken-hearted were mended; and the captives were set free. And today you and I can never get the real pulse beat back into the life of the church or see any sense whatever to our coming together on Sunday morning unless our worship is motivated by praise to God for the victories of his kingdom we witnessed during the past week.

III

Now a third, and final observation: *the rediscovery of praise goes hand in hand with service.*

One of the most impressive features of the regular service of worship in many of our churches is the opening processional of the choir and the leaders of worship down the center aisle of the nave and into the chancel. It is impressive because it has its own meaning and significance. It is not just a handy means by which to get the choristers and the ministers in. Its symbolism is well expressed in a poetic couplet by Von Ogden Vogt:

> Up from the world of the many
> To the over-world of the One.

This processional is all the more thrilling when the choir enters singing one of the great hymns of praise of the Christian church. Some of us have worshiped in St. Columba Scottish Kirk in London, England, and have been moved by the great processional entering and singing:

> Ye gates, lift up your heads on high;
> Ye doors that last for aye,
> Be lifted up, that so the King
> Of Glory enter may.

We must not, however, think of this processional as merely a unilateral act; it embraces the whole congregation and includes the whole community. Remember that disturbing item in the Sermon on the Mount where Jesus is talking about our coming into the temple to worship and suddenly he delivers the real crunch when he says: "If you are about to offer your gift to God at the altar and there you remember that your brother has something against you, leave your gift there in front of the altar, go at once and make peace with your brother, and then come back and offer your gift to God" (Matt. 5:23–24, T.E.V.). Now Jesus did not mean that the patching up of a quarrel was a substitute for praise. That activist heresy has never found a permanent base. He meant that praise goes hand in hand with moral and social responsibility. And you and I know that responsibility begets service. Praise can never be an insulated matter. There is no such thing as solitary praise anymore than there being any sense to a single person saluting the flag all alone in the town square at six o'clock in the morning.

Years ago I used to attend in the summer a church camp for teenagers and among the memories that remain vividly with me is the evening campfire and the sing-song on the hillside above the lake. Always as the shadows were deepening and the red embers were dying, the song leader would direct us in that haunting Negro spiritual, "We Are Climbing Jacob's Ladder." Softly under the starlit heavens we concluded:

> If you love Him why not serve Him?
> If you love Him why not serve Him?
> If you love Him why not serve Him?
> Soldiers of the Cross!

How much did these words echo the experience of Isaiah in the temple. There he heard the heavenly choir sing its praise to God: "Holy, holy, holy, Lord God of hosts. Heaven and earth are full of thy glory. Glory be to thee, O Lord most high!" But this overture of praise was not an isolated act; it emerged in a contract of service. "Here am I," said the prophet, "send me." So will our every act of worship each Sunday morning become a rare and tremendous experience if on Monday, Tuesday, Wednesday, Thursday, Friday, and Saturday we shall paraphrase in our hearts the words of this ethnic song:

> If you love Him why not *praise* Him?
> If you praise Him why not *serve* Him?
> Soldiers of the Cross!

2: Something Happened in Church

*As for me, my feet were almost gone; my steps had
well nigh slipped ... until I went into the sanctuary
of God; then understood I...*

Psalm 73:2, 17 (k.j.v.)

One day at the seminary in a class discussion on worship,
a rather perceptive student made this remark, "Long ago
when you came home from church, people would ask 'Who
was there?' or 'What was the sermon about?' Today, however,
they are more apt to say, 'Well, you were in church this morning, what happened?'"

Some years ago Henrik Kraemer of Geneva wrote as follows: "Every Christian needs two conversions: the first to
Christ; the second to the world." Now in several ways Kraemer was entirely right. Often you and I are surprised by the
number of people we meet who have been converted only
to the world—the busy people in the welfare agencies and the
PTA or on the political fronts and among the pressure
groups—but who have never been converted to Christ. On
the other hand, we are not so easily disturbed by the number
of people who have been converted to Christ, but never to the
world: the priests and the Levites on the Jericho Road or the
clergy in John Milton's seventeenth century England of
whom he wrote, "The hungry sheep look up, but are not fed."
Kraemer was right also in using the word *convert* rather than
reconcile, because to reconcile oneself to something or someone can mean merely to resign oneself to it or to make the
best of a situation or even to grin and bear it. However, he
was particularly right in putting conversion to God (or Christ)
and to the world together, because they are parts of one event

*Preached in the Riverside Church, New York City.

and because no devotion to God is worth much unless it includes also conversion to the claims of humanity.

Our text comes from Psalm 73. This psalm is the story of a
religious Jew who had reconciled himself to the world in a
negative sort of way and of how this affected his conception of
God and of how God was running things. He was a good man
in the conventional sense of the term, but his outlook upon
the world and life drove him into a fit of doubt and skepti-
cism; he was confused and all mixed up. He looked out upon
his community, and what he saw shook his soul: wicked men,
prospering and successful, striding arrogantly across the stage
of life as if the world were theirs alone. Spineless "do-
gooders" trying by flattery and flunky-ism to cash in upon
gains they had never earned. On every hand, goodness was
persecuted, inequality flaunted, fairness flouted, and with
James R. Lowell, he might have said, "Truth forever on the
scaffold, wrong forever on the throne"—Watergate, Chappa-
quiddick, nursing-home scandals, judgeships gained through
bribes—and like an angry person he was about to jettison his
faith. He doubted the integrity of God and was skeptical regarding the dependability of people; indeed before the bar of
his own judgment, both seemed to be wanting. He felt his
grip on God was breaking and in a sour, peevish bit of temper
he was ready to write the world off as the victim of blind fate.
There were no rewards for goodness and the prizes went inevitably to scoundrels. All this was too much for him. Seemingly he cried out, "Is there anyone at all in charge here?"

But then in something for a spur-of-the-moment decision,
when his "feet were almost gone" and his "steps had well
nigh slipped," he went into the sanctuary of God and there,
once and for all, he understood. Now we have no knowledge
of what actually occurred, but we do know the psalmist
gained a new perspective upon things, and he began to see
the world and life in God's context and not his own. In the
sanctuary he put himself where God could get at him more
effectively and have some chance with him. And from then
and there on he could face Monday through Saturday a differ-

ent person because he was straightened out spiritually, because his perspective went through a radical reorientation, and because he was converted to both God *and* the world. Life was no longer a moral chaos or a jumble of things going it blind, but something God-centered and God-controlled. "As for me my feet were almost gone; my steps had well nigh slipped . . . until I went into the sanctuary of God, then I understood. . . ."

I

Something happened in church—and the first thing the psalmist learned was the simple, age-old principle that what a person is and not what he or she has is what counts.

Up to this point, however, the psalmist had had his doubts, because as he looked out upon the earth, it were as if God had abandoned it or rather as though there were no God at all. The wicked were the haves and the good the have-nots. Six days a week he saw life admired for, and equated with, those things men and women could see or flaunt or grab. And success was measured, not in terms of involvement or saintliness or service, but by the power of one's clout or by big wheels making big deals over big meals. And God seemed to stand idly by. Sounds familiar, doesn't it? Are we talking about 1980 B.C. or A.D. 1980?

Some years ago, Dr. E. Stanley Jones, the great Christian missionary to India, was speaking to a large audience of American young people, and he declared, "You have everything; you are a much better generation than mine, better trained and two inches taller; but you lack one thing—you lack a cause!" And a young man arose and interrupted him, saying, "But, Dr. Jones, we have a cause!" "What is it?" asked Jones. "To succeed," came the reply. A newspaper man, who was present, remarked to a colleague, "What a magnificent answer!" But he was wrong, dead wrong! It was a tragic answer, because that young boy meant only more power, more prosperity, more know-how, and more things. He was very much like a brash young man who turned to his future father-in-law on the eve of his engagement to his daughter and snapped, "I make three hundred bucks a week; what do you care whether or not I've got a character?"

But then you and I go to church and there we hear of the greatest person who ever lived, who cleft history in twain and left his stamp forever on human destiny; that this man—Jesus of Nazareth—led an amazing life, not measured in terms of investments and dividends, but in quality of spirit. He showed men and women the real things to live by, the prescription by which to become truly human, and his focus was consistently upon what a person is rather than upon what he or she has. His was a vision that claimed people's energies; a faith that gripped their imagination; a cause for them not only to live for, but also to die for, because neither is worthwhile without the other. This is what you and I find in church. A new dimension to life opens up before us, and we go out into the hurly-burly of the world, not saying, "This belongs to me" or "That belongs to me," but because of who I am in God's sight and of what I have from God's hand, I belong *to* this world and accept moral responsibility in it and for it. An old missionary shrank from the sight of the foreign field with its contradictions of everything he ever knew, yet in the sanctuary of his devotion he prayed, "There let me burn out for God." The psalmist declared at length: "Whom have I in heaven but thee? And there is none on earth I desire beside thee." This is not a matter of having or getting, but of being on the side of right as God gives us the ability to discern the right; and no one is greater than when he or she is possessed by God.

II

Something happened in church—and the second thing the psalmist learned was that the best way to handle wrong is to witness to what is true and right.

How very much the world of the psalmist resembles ours! People in those days were caught up in the world of fancy, of sham, and of make-believe; and somehow they liked it. It had something of a romantic flavor about it, although underneath lay the grim, dog-eat-dog way of life. Life as they lived it was paying off; therefore let us not rock the boat. We have never had it so good!

But the psalmist was disillusioned by what he saw. He witnessed the false crowding out the true, and the growing number of persons without any convictions who were ready to join any bandwagon as long as it was rolling. He wondered if God were asleep or whether he just did not care. So he was ready to quit. But then he went into the sanctuary of God, and there he saw reflections of real goodness, real purity, and real truth. Before him the hidden wrongs were exposed of what had become a popular and synthetic way of life, and there he saw, etched in clear outline, an image of the true and right.

Something happened in church—and is not this the risk all of us take every time we come here to worship? Often we wonder why many people today do not come to church. But have you and I ever thought that more people than we imagine are *frightened* to come to church? What do we mean? People who are satisfied with the slogan, "Anything goes," will avoid the church because it confronts them with facts that disturb and irritate them. They do not want to be reminded of the claims of truth, duty, love to God, and charity towards others. It is much easier to live by a philosophy of positive thinking that makes no demand beyond saying every morning before the mirror: "Every day and in every way I am getting better and better." It is much easier to talk about love of the synthetic kind which is paraded by the soap operas on the national television networks than it is to gaze on real love which dies on a cross. In church you and I come up against real virtues and God asks: "What is your personal relationship to these?" In church we encounter the eternal cleavage between right and wrong, love and hate, truth and falsehood.

It is just here that it is appropriate to say a word in defense of mass evangelism. Some people claim it has had its day and that the Grahams and Leighton Fords are as dated as the

Model T. However, in an age in which the mass media has captured public opinion and popularized the shabby side of sex, the dividends of violence, and the notion that a certain brand of deodorant is the key to personal success, maybe it is for our nation's good that these religious mass rallies become symbols of human witness to the integrity of goodness and truth. Indeed, this church, as well as all other churches and chapels across the land today, is a sanctuary, like an oasis in our political and cultural deserts, testifying before men and women that above all truths there is THE TRUTH that saves and redeems.

III

Something happened in church—and this brings us to a final point: the psalmist saw himself not only as he had been, but particularly as what, by God's grace he could become.

One Sunday some years ago I preached at the twenty-fifth anniversary of the ordination of one of the alumni of Princeton Theological Seminary. I had given the sermon originally at his ordination on May 24, 1951. Few men I know have gone through greater tragedies and more sorry disappointments than he has; yet he isn't bitter, nor defiant, nor complaining. Moreover, in the service of worship that morning he took a few moments to talk to his people about the goodness and loving-kindness of God. Nowhere else but in the sanctuary of God could he have talked in this way, and be understood; nowhere else is the knowledge and experience of the strong hand of God preserved and permitted to bring men and women to such splendid hours. "As for me," said the psalmist, "my feet were almost gone, my steps had well nigh slipped, until I went into the sanctuary of God, then I understood. . . ."

William Temple, the celebrated Archbishop of Canterbury in the 1940s said: "This world can be saved from political chaos and collapse by one thing only, that is worship. For to worship is to devote the will to the purpose of God."

As the psalmist left the sanctuary that day, he knew he was not alone, because he felt led by a hand and held by a power not his own. He was no longer against God or against the world, but he was converted to both. William M. Macgregor of Glasgow once said, "When a man comes to God, it were as if he looked from the other side of the sky, seeing the same things from another standpoint." That happened to the psalmist in church.

In the little village of Blantyre, Scotland, a common laborer by the name of David Hogg taught a small Sunday school class of young boys year after year with a devotion that was the wonder of all who knew him. Out from that class went a young man, David Livingstone, to the vast continent of Africa to wear out his life, going through the jungles from village to village, witnessing to the Christian faith. Some time later another missionary came to one of these same villages where Livingstone had been years before, and he told of the life and ministry of Jesus Christ. An old lady, however, interrupted him and said, "That man has been here!"

Think of it, men and women: a village church in far away Scotland; a little boy in the sanctuary; a consecrated Sunday school teacher; and you get the footprints of Christ in and out of the muddy villages of Africa.

Something happened in church!

May our prayer today be:

O God, do it again!
And again! And again!

GLOSSARY

Acolyte:
> In episcopal traditions usually a young boy who assists the priest at the altar. In Presbyterian churches he does little more than light and extinguish the candles near the communion table.

Agape:
> One of the New Testament words for love (the others: *eros* and *philia*). It refers to the early Christian love feast, a service held in conjunction with a celebration of the Eucharist. (Pronounced ah-GAH-pay).

Agnus Dei:
> The Latin for "Lamb of God." Taken from John 1:29, it refers to a seventh-century chant used just prior to receiving the elements in Holy Communion.

Alleluia:
> A Hebrew term meaning "Praise ye Jehovah," borrowed unchanged by the Christian church.

Alpha and Omega:
> The first and last letters of the Greek alphabet. In Revelation 1:8, they symbolize the eternal divinity of Christ and through the ages they have been used on furnishings and facades in churches.

Amen:
> A Hebrew term for "So be it" or "verily." It is used at the end of prayers and praises to indicate approval or assent.

Antependium:
> A Latin term meaning "hanging before." It refers to the cloth which hangs on the front of the pulpit or lectern.

Antiphonal:
> A method of singing responsively between two sides of a chancel choir or between minister and choir.

Apse:
>A semicircular area at the east end of a church where the communion table is located.

Ascription:
>A brief doxology given by the minister at the close of a sermon or prayer.

Banns:
>The proclamation in church of an intended marriage. It is optional in some countries, required in others.

Benediction:
>The pronouncement of God's blessing upon the congregation at the close of the service of worship.

Canon:
>In Reformed churches, canon means the list of genuine and inspired books in the Bible.

Canticle:
>Means "a little song" and is taken usually from the Scriptures, e.g., The Magnificat (Luke 1:46–55).

Carillon:
>A set of specially tuned and graded bells in a church tower, played by an electric keyboard by a trained musician known as a carillonneur.

Chalice:
>A cup, usually silver, used for sacramental wine during the consecration.

Chancel:
>Located at the east end of the church and raised by three steps above the level of the nave, it may contain communion table, organ console, and choir stalls.

Collect:
>The word comes from the Latin *collectio* meaning "to sum up" and is the name of a brief prayer that sums up the thought or significance of the day or season.

Confiteor:
>A prayer in which a confession of sin is made.

Créche:
>A small crib or manger as part of a Nativity scene at Christmas time.

Cruciform:
>A design in the form or shape of a cross.

Dossal:
>A curtain of silk or tapestry which is hung on the east wall of the chancel and behind the communion table.

Ecumenical:
> From the Greek word *oikoumene,* meaning "world-wide" or "the whole inhabited earth."

Eucharist:
> Coming from the Greek word εὐχαριστία, meaning "Thanksgiving," it was an early name for the Lord's Supper.

Gloria in Excelsis:
> A doxology used by the church as early as the fourth century. Originating from Luke 2:13, it has been known as the Great Doxology ("Glory be to God on high").

Gloria Patri:
> A short doxology, "Glory be to the Father ... Son ... Holy Ghost," used after a Psalm as an ascription to the Trinity.

Gloria Tibi:
> An ascription given by the people immediately before the reading of the Gospel lesson.

IHS:
> The first three letters of the Greek word for Jesus.

I.N.R.I.:
> The initials of the Latin wording of the inscription Pilate set upon the cross, "Jesus of Nazareth, King of the Jews."

Kyrie Eleison:
> Greek form of "Lord, have mercy upon us," an early petition of both Eastern and Western churches.

Lectern:
> A stand upon which the Bible is placed and from which the Scripture lessons are read.

Lectionary:
> A formal listing of Scripture lessons according to the structure of the Christian Year.

Litany:
> A form of prayer in which the word of thanksgiving or petition is given by the minister and the responses made in unison by the congregation.

Magnificat:
> Taken from Luke 1:46–55, it is the song of Mary after the announcement to her of the coming of the Christ child. The name comes from the opening word of praise, "My soul *magnifies* the Lord ..."

Manse:
> The home provided for and occupied by Presbyterian clergy.

Narthex:
> The vestibule or closed-in porch of a church.

Nave:
> The main body of the church where congregation is seated. The early church was compared to the "ark of God" or ship (Latin: *navis*).

Nunc Dimittis:
> Taken from Luke 2:29–32, the song of the aged Simeon, it is used as a short evening hymn.

Offertory:
> The act of collecting and presenting the gifts of the people as response in worship.

Reredos:
> A screen or decorated panel behind the communion table.

Rubric:
> Inserted directions for the conduct of the various parts of the act of worship were usually printed in red ink. Hence rubric from the Latin *ruber* and the French *rubrique.*

Sanctuary:
> In Reformed churches it is the main room for worship; in the Episcopal tradition it is the area where the altar stands.

Tenebrae:
> Taken from the Latin word for "darkness," it is a service of mourning embracing the last three days of Holy Week and symbolizes the darkness over the earth during the crucifixion. Fifteen candles are lighted and extinguished progressively until only one is left.

Transept:
> The north and south arms of the cruciform designed church. Where they intersect the nave is called the crossing.

Triptych:
> Coming from the Greek word meaning "threefold," the name is given to three hinged panels of a painting or carving behind an altar.

Vespers:
> A name given to evening worship, but originally was one of the canonical hours (at sunset).

Vestry:
> In a Presbyterian church it is a room where the minister robes and prepares for the service.

NOTES

CHAPTER ONE

1. John Huxtable, *The Bible Says* (Richmond: John Knox Press, 1962), p. 109.
2. Study Guide for *The Directory for Worship* (Philadelphia: United Presbyterian Church, U.S.A., 1964), p. 7.
3. Richard Davidson, "The Worship of the Reformed Churches," *The Presbyterian Register*, Vol. XVII, No. 10, p. 292.
4. John G. Williams, *Worship and the Modern Child: A Book for Parents, Clergy, and Teachers* (London: SPCK, 1957), p. 18.
5. *The Directory for Worship*, II, §2, *The Book of Order* (New York: United Presbyterian Church, U.S.A., 1978). Used with permission.
6. Vilmos Vajta, "The Theological Basis and Nature of the Liturgy," *Lutheran World*, Vol. VI, No. 3, p. 234.
7. J. D. Benoit in *Liturgical Renewal: Studies in Catholic and Protestant Developments on the Continent* (London: SCM Press, 1958), p. 59.
8. *The United Church Observer*, XXIV (n.s.), No. 8, p. 21.
9. Romans 12:1.
10. Neville Clark, *Call to Worship* (London: SCM Press, 1960), p. 38.
11. Davidson, "The Worship of the Reformed Churches," p. 292.
12. Clark, *Call to Worship*, pp. 38–39.
13. Massey H. Shepherd, Jr. (ed.), *The Liturgical Renewal of the Church* (New York: Oxford University Press, 1960), p. 102.
14. Willard L. Sperry, *Reality in Worship* (New York: The Macmillan Co., 1925), p. 168.
15. Quoted by Alfred R. Shands in *The Liturgical Movement and the Local Church* (London: SCM Press, 1959), p. 27.
16. Hans J. Rinderknecht, "Laymen and Reformed Worship," *The Reformed and Presbyterian World*, Vol. XXIV, No. 5, p. 158.

17. Eduard Schweizer, "Worship in the New Testament," *The Reformed and Presbyterian World*, Vol. XXIV, No. 5, p. 199.

18. Paul Jacobs, "The Holy Spirit and the Development of Thought in the Modern Period down to Existentialism," *The Reformed and Presbyterian World*, Vol. XXVII, No. 2, p. 63.

19. William D. Maxwell, *An Outline of Christian Worship: Its Development and Forms* (New York: Oxford University Press, 1958), p. 116.

20. E. Doumergue, *Jean Calvin* (Lausanne: G. Bridel, 1902), Vol. II, p. 504.

21. Eduard Thurneysen, "The Biblical and Dogmatic Foundation of Pastoral Theology," *The Reformed and Presbyterian World*, Vol. XXV, No. 3, p. 111.

22. Cf. J.R.P. Sclater, *The Public Worship of God* (New York: George H. Doran Co., 1927), pp. 29–33; *The Book of Common Worship*, The Church of South India (London: Oxford University Press, 1963), pp. 5–8; and Thomas H. Keir, *The Word in Worship: Preaching and Its Setting in Common Worship* (New York: Oxford University Press, 1962), pp. 145–146.

23. Quoted by A. G. Reynolds in *The Living Church* (Toronto: Ryerson Press, 1949), p. 92.

24. Raymond Abba, *Principles of Christian Worship: With Special Reference to the Free Churches* (New York: Oxford University Press, 1960), p. 103.

25. *In the Secret Place of the Most High* (New York: Scribner's, 1947), p. 16.

26. William D. Maxwell, *Concerning Worship* (London: Oxford University Press, 1948), p. 31.

27. Bard Thompson, *Liturgies of the Western Church* (Cleveland, Ohio: The World Publishing Co., 1961), p. 191.

28. *The Directory for Worship*, IV, §6. Cf. *The Directory for the Worship and Work of the Church* (Richmond: Board of Christian Education, Presbyterian Church, U.S., 1963), §204–1. Used with permission.

29. Schweizer, "Worship in the New Testament," p. 205.

30. *The Directory for Worship*, IV, §6.

31. Cf. Henry Sloane Coffin, *The Public Worship of God* (Philadelphia: The Westminster Press, 1946), p. 101.

32. *The Directory for Worship*, IV, §3.

33. John Marsh in *Ways of Worship*, ed. P. Edwall, E. Hayman, & W. D. Maxwell (New York: Harper and Brothers, 1951), p. 154.

34. *The Directory for Worship*, IV, §8; also *The Worshipbook* (Philadelphia: The Westminster Press, 1972), pp. 28–29.

35. Charles Cuthbert Hall, *Christian Worship* (New York: Charles Scribner's Sons, 1896), p. 15.
36. *Ibid.*, p. 179.
37. Dom Gregory Dix, *The Shape of the Liturgy* (Westminster, England: Dacre Press, 1949), p. 37.
38. *The Directory for Worship*, IV, §9.
39. P. T. Forsyth, *Positive Preaching and the Modern Mind* (Grand Rapids: Eerdmans, 1964), p. 53.
40. William Temple, *The Hope of a New World* (New York: The Macmillan Co., 1942), pp. 26–27.

CHAPTER TWO

1. *The Book of Common Order*, The Presbyterian Church in Canada (Toronto: Presbyterian Publications, 1964), p. 218.
2. Frank Colquhoun, *Contemporary Parish Prayers* (London: Hodder & Stoughton, 1975), p. 213.
3. *The Book of Common Order*, The Church of Scotland (London: Oxford University Press, 1962), p. 3. Used by courtesy of the Church of Scotland Committee on Public Worship.
4. Colquhoun, *Contemporary Parish Prayers*, p. 234.
5. Donald D. Kettring, *Steps Toward a Singing Church* (Philadelphia: The Westminster Press, 1948), p. 277.
6. Sclater, *The Public Worship of God*, p. 30.
7. Suggested passages from Scripture: Psalm 95:6,7; Psalm 100; Psalm 145:18,19; Isaiah 1:18; Isaiah 35:6,7; Habakkuk 2:20; Matthew 7:7,8; Matthew 11:28–30; Matthew 18:19; Luke 1:78,79; Philippians 4:6,7; Hebrews 10:19,20.
8. Coffin, *The Public Worship of God*, p. 98.
9. Scott Francis Brenner, *The Art of Worship: A Guide in Corporate Worship Techniques* (New York: The Macmillan Co., 1961), p. 23.
10. Rupert Sircom, *The Diapason* (Nov. 1, 1943), p. 21.
11. *Book of Common Order*, Church of Scotland, p. 30.
12. *Book of Common Worship* (Philadelphia: United Presbyterian Church, U.S.A., 1946), pp. 46–47.
13. *Service Book*, The United Church of Canada (Toronto: The Ryerson Press, 1969), p. 111.
14. *The Directory for Worship*, IV, §5.
15. For further discussion of the Preparation, see *The Living Church*, ed. by H. W. Vaughan (Toronto: Ryerson Press, 1949), p. 97; *Worship: A Study of Corporate Devotion* by Luther D. Reed (Philadel-

phia: Fortress Press, 1959), p. 76; and *An Experimental Liturgy* by G. F. Cope, J. G. Davies, and D. A. Tytler (Richmond: John Knox Press, 1958), pp. 11, 30–31.

16. *The Worshipbook: Services and Hymns* (Philadelphia: Westminster, 1970, 72) p. 28.

17. Coffin, *The Public Worship of God*, p. 101.

18. A. S. Peake, *Commentary on the Bible* (London: Thomas Nelson & Sons, 1962).

19. Richard C. White, *The Vocabulary of the Church: A Pronunciation Guide* (New York: The Macmillan Co., 1960).

20. Wilhelm Hahn, *Worship and Congregation:* Ecumenical Studies in Worship, No. 12 (Richmond: John Knox Press, 1963), p. 50.

21. *Ibid.*

22. *The Directory for Worship*, IV; §3.

23. *The Directory for the Worship and Work of the Church*, §207–2.

24. *The Directory for Worship*, IV, §8.

25. Donald Tytler, "The Experimental Liturgy with Commentary and an Appended Note" in *An Experimental Liturgy*, p. 35.

26. *The Directory for Worship*, IV, §10.

27. George S. Stewart, "The Moods of Christian Worship" in *The Expository Times*, LI, p. 138.

28. *The Directory for Worship*, IV, §7. Cf. *The Directory for the Worship and Work of the Church*, §§207–1, 203–4.

29. *Ibid*, III, §3.

30. *Ibid.*

31. Davidson, "The Worship of the Reformed Churches," p. 290.

32. Reuel Howe, "Overcoming Barriers to Communication," *The Princeton Seminary Bulletin*, LVI, p. 52.

33. T. H. Keir, *The Word in Worship* (New York: Oxford University Press, 1962), p. 41.

34. Paul Tillich in *Union Seminary Review*, VII, 5, p. 10.

35. Jean-Jacques von Allmen, *Preaching and Congregation:* Ecumenical Studies in Worship, No. 10 (Richmond: John Knox Press, 1962), p. 41.

CHAPTER THREE

1. *The Sacraments* (Madras: The Christian Literature Society, 1956), p. 1.

2. *The Directory for Worship*, III, §3. Also *The Directory for the Worship and Work of the Church*, IX (209:1–9).

3. Ronald S. Wallace, *Calvin's Doctrine of the Word and Sacrament*

(Edinburgh: Oliver & Boyd, 1953), p. 150.

4. J. A. Davidson, "Getting Little Nellie Done," *The United Church Observer*, XIX, (n.s.), No 7, pp. 12–13.

5. Emil Brunner, *The Divine-Human Encounter* Philadelphia: The Westminster Press, 1943), pp. 181–183.

6. W. F. Flemington, *The New Testament Doctrine of Baptism* (London: SPCK, 1948), p. 134.

7. P. T. Forsyth, *The Church and the Sacraments* (London: Independent Press Ltd., 1947), pp. 216, 220.

8. *The Directory for Worship*, V, §1.

9. *Studies in the Ministry and Worship*, No. 17 (London: SCM Press, 1961), p. 56.

10. George S. Hendry, *The Westminster Confession for Today* (Richmond: John Knox Press, 1960), p. 227.

11. H. W. Vaughan (ed.), *The Living Church* (Toronto: Ryerson Press, 1949), p. 105.

12. Davidson, "The Worship of the Reformed Churches," p. 292.

13. Hugh Thompson Kerr, *The Christian Sacraments: A Source Book for Ministers* (Philadelphia: The Westminster Press, 1944), p. 59.

14. Richard Davidson, "The Church: Its Sacraments" in *The Living Church*, ed. by Harold W. Vaughan (Toronto: The United Church Publishing House, 1949), p. 112.

15. Kerr, *The Christian Sacraments*, p. 34.

16. *Ibid.*, pp. 69–70.

17. Davidson. "The Church: Its Sacraments." p. 34.

18. James Hastings (ed.), *Encyclopedia of Religion and Ethics*, Vol. II (New York: Charles Scribner's Sons, 1910), p. 379.

19. John Dow, *This Is Our Faith* (Toronto: The United Church Publishing House, 1943), p. 192.

20. Kerr, *The Christian Sacraments*, p. 54.

21. *The Directory for Worship*, V, §3.

22. James Barr, "Further Thoughts About Baptism," *Scottish Journal of Theology*, Vol. IV, No. 3, p. 268.

23. Jeremiah 1:5.

24. Emile Cailliet and John Blankenagel (trans.), *Great Shorter Works of Pascal* (Philadelphia: The Westminster Press, 1948), p. 135.

25. *The Book of Common Order* of The United Church of Canada (1932 edition), pp. 98–99.

26. Forsyth, *The Church and Its Sacraments*, p. 177.

27. *The Directory for Worship*, V, §1. *The Directory for the Worship and Work of the Church*, IX, §3.

28. Flemington, *The New Testament Doctrine of Baptism*, p. 143.
29. *The Book of Common Worship*, The Church of South India (London: Oxford University Press, 1963), pp. 117–118.
30. Cf. *The Directory for the Worship and Work of the Church*, §209–5.
31. Interim Report on the Biblical Doctrine of Baptism (The Church of Scotland, 1958), p. 18.
32. *Ibid.*, p. 18.

CHAPTER FOUR

1. Wallace, *Calvin's Doctrine of the Word and Sacrament*, p. 154.
2. Walter Lüthi, "The Lord's Supper in the Local Congregation" in *Preaching, Confession, The Lord's Supper*, trans. Francis J. Brooke, III (Richmond: John Knox Press, 1960), pp. 81, 83.
3. Wilhelm Niesel, *The Theology of Calvin*, trans. Harold Knight (Philadelphia: The Westminster Press, 1956), pp. 212–213.
4. *Ibid.*, p. 215.
5. Baum, Cunitz, and Reuss (eds.), *Corpus Reformatorum*, Vol. IX.
6. John Calvin, *The Institutes of the Christian Religion* (Grand Rapids: W. B. Eerdmans, 1953), IV, xvii, 39, p. 596.
7. J. S. Whale, *Christian Doctrine* (New York: Cambridge University Press, 1963), p. 161.
8. Hendry, *The Westminster Confession for Today*, p. 233.
9. D. H. Hislop, *Our Heritage in Public Worship* (Edinburgh: T & T. Clark, 1936), pp. 184, 186.
10. Wallace, *Calvin's Doctrine of the Word and Sacrament*, p. 150.
11. *The Directory for Worship*, IV, §3.
12. Nathaniel Micklem (ed.), *Christian Worship* (New York: Oxford University Press, 1936), p. 252.
13. Donald M. Baillie, *The Theology of the Sacraments: And Other Papers* (New York: Charles Scribner's Sons, 1957), p. 39.
14. *Ibid.*, p. 40.
15. *The Directory for Worship*, VI, §3.
16. Abba, *Principles of Christian Worship*, p. 154.
17. A. M. Hunter, *The Teaching of Calvin: A Modern Interpretation* (London: James Clark & Co., 1950), p. 168.
18. *The Directory for Worship*, VI, §1.
19. *Ibid.*, VI, §3.
20. Robert Bruce, *The Mystery of the Lord's Supper*, trans. and ed. by Thomas F. Torrance (Richmond: John Knox Press, 1958), p. 85.
21. *The Sacraments*, p. 41.
22. Based upon *The Directory for Worship*, VI, §4; and *The Directory for the Worship and Work of the Church*, 11.

23. Cf. D. Dr. Joachim Jeremias, *The Eucharistic Words of Jesus,* trans. Arnold Ehrhardt (New York: The Macmillan Co., 1955), pp. 38–40.

24. Cf. *An Experimental Liturgy* by Cope, Davies, and Tytler; also Brenner, *The Art of Worship,* pp. 40, 46.

25. Kerr, *The Christian Sacraments,* pp. 98, 105.

26. Oswald Milligan, *The Ministry of Worship* (London: Oxford University Press, 1941), p. 113.

27. "The Doctrine of Infant Baptism" by Commission on Christian Faith (Toronto: United Church of Canada, 1954), p. 8.

28. Report of Committee on Revision of *The Book of Common Order,* Presbyterian Church in Canada, 1957.

CHAPTER FIVE

1. *The New York Times,* July 1, 1979.

2. *The Directory for Worship,* VII, §2; *The Directory for the Worship and Work of the Church,* §215–7.

3. See Massey Hamilton Shepherd, Jr., *The Oxford American Prayer Book Commentary* (New York: Oxford University Press, 1950), pp. 300–303, for short history of the marriage ceremony.

4. Frederick W. Brink, *This Man and This Woman: A Guide for Those Contemplating Marriage* (New York: Association Press, 1948), p. 18.

5. Kenneth J. Foreman, *From This Day Forward* (Richmond: Outlook Publishers, 1950), p. 18.

6. Brink, *This Man and This Woman,* p. 33.

7. H. Grady Hardin, Joseph D. Quillan, Jr., James F. White, *The Celebration of the Gospel: A Study in Christian Worship* (Nashville: Abingdon Press, 1964), p. 138.

8. Joseph E. McCabe, *Service Book for Ministers* (New York: McGraw-Hill Book Co., 1961), p. 116.

9. Khoren Arisian, *The New Wedding* (New York: Random House, 1973), p. 69.

10. *Ibid.,* p. 40.

11. See Wedding Bulletin by Sacred Design Associates, Box 5452, Minneapolis, Minnesota.

CHAPTER SIX

1. R. C. Chalmers (ed.), *The Minister's Handbook* (Toronto: United Church Publishing House, 1952), p. 147.

2. Von Ogden Vogt in *The Christian Century*, LXII, No. 12, p. 362.

3. Roy A. Burkhart, "The Service of Memory," *Pastoral Psychology*, Vol. 1, No. 5, p. 22.

4. Joseph E. McCabe, *The Power of God in a Parish Program* (Philadelphia: The Westminster Press, 1959), p. 73.

5. See Old and New Testament selections in *The Book of Common Worship*, pp. 193–212.

6. *The Book of Common Worship* (1946 edition), p. 364.

7. From a brochure, "The Christian Funeral" (prepared by the Session of the Union Presbyterian Church of Bay Ridge, New York. George C. Bonnell, minister.)

8. Cf. Walter E. Schuette, *The Minister's Personal Guide* (New York: Harper and Brothers, 1953), p. 45.

9. Lowell H. Zuch, "The Changing Meaning of the Funeral in Christian History," *Pastoral Psychology*, Vol. VIII, No. 78, p. 17.

10. *Music for Church Funerals* (Greenwich: Seabury Press, 1952).

CHAPTER SEVEN

1. Charles H. Heimsath, *The Genius of Public Worship* (New York: Charles Scribner's Sons, 1947), p. 149.

2. Allan Hauck, *Calendar of Christianity* (New York: Association Press, 1961), p. 28.

3. "The First Apology of Justin," *Ante-Nicene Fathers* (Grand Rapids: Wm. B. Eerdmans, 1953), Vol. 1, LXVII, p. 186.

4. Constantine, "State Recognition of Sunday, 321" *Documents of the Christian Church*, ed. by Henry Bettenson (New York: Oxford University Press, 1947), p. 27.

5. Kirsopp Lake (ed.), "The Epistle of Barnabas" in *The Apostolic Fathers* (Loeb Classical Library, Cambridge: Harvard University Press, 1959). Vol. 1, 15, pp. 395–397.

6. Pliny, *Letters*, ed. by W. M. L. Hutchinson (Loeb Classical Library, New York: MacMillan, 1915), Vol, II, pp. 403–405.

7. Quoted by Mgr. L. Duchesne in *Christian Worship: Its Origin and Evolution* (London: SPCK, 1931), pp. 543–544.

8. A. Allan McArthur, *The Evolution of the Christian Year* (London: SCM Press, 1953), p. 20.

9. Dix, *The Shape of the Liturgy*, p. 336.

10. Cf. C. H. Dodd, *The Apostolic Preaching and Its Developments* (London: Hodder & Stoughton, 1944).

11. Hauck, *Calendar of Christianity*, p. 56.

12. F. E. Wilson, *An Outline of the Christian Year* (New York: Morehouse-Gorham Co., 1960), p. 55.

13. Collect, First Sunday After Trinity *(Book of Common Prayer).*
14. Wilson, *An Outline of the Christian Year,* p. 81.
15. Cf. *The Handbook for Presbyterians* (Plan Book for 1963–64), 475 Riverside Drive, New York, New York, 10027.
16. A. Allan McArthur, *The Christian Year and Lectionary Reform* (London: SCM Press, 1958).
17. *Service for the Lord's Day and Lectionary for the Christian Year* (Philadelphia: Westminster, 1964). p. 45.

CHAPTER EIGHT

1. *The Directory for Worship,* IV, §3. Also *The Directory for the Worship and Work of the Church,* I:5 (205:1–3)
2. Austin C. Lovelace and William C. Rice, *Music and Worship in the Church* (Nashville: Abingdon Press, 1960), p. 40.
3. *Ibid.,* p. 41.
4. George Hedley, *Christian Worship: Some Meanings and Means* (New York: The Macmillan Co., 1953), p. 68.
5. *Ibid.,* p. 71.
6. See William McMillan, *The Worship of the Scottish Reformed Church: 1550–1638* (Edinburgh: Lassodie Press, 1931), p. 364.
7. Reed, *Worship,* pp. 302–303.
8. Brenner, *The Art of Worship,* p. 71.
9. Reed, *Worship,* p. 307.
10. McMillan, *The Worship of the Scottish Reformed Church: 1550–1638,* p. 365.
11. Nathaniel Micklem, *Congregationalism and the Church Catholic* (London: Independent Press, 1944).
12. Cf. Sacred Design, Concordia Publishing House, St. Louis, Missouri.
13. Gilbert Cope (ed.), *Making the Building Serve the Liturgy* (London: A. R. Mowbray, 1962), p. 11.
14. *Briefs for Church Builders,* No. 20 (National Council of Churches), p. 2.
15. J. G. Davies, "Baptismal Architecture" in *The Modern Architectural Setting of the Liturgy,* ed. William Lockett (London: SPCK, 1964), p. 2.
16. *Ibid.*
17. James H. Nichols and Leonard J. Trinterud, *The Architectural Setting for Reformed Worship* (Presbytery of Chicago, 1960), p. 20.
18. John Stewart Detlie, "A Religious Architecture for Today," *Religious Buildings for Today* (New York: Dodge, 1937), p. 174.

CHAPTER NINE

1. Cf. *The Book of Church Order*, The Presbyterian Church in the U.S., 1977–78, Part 5, Chapters 23 ff., especially 27 on "The Ordination and Installation of Ministers."

2. See his exegetical commentary, *The Epistle to the Philippians* (London: Macmillan and Co., 1878), pp. 181–269. (Other useful monographs are T. W. Manson, *The Church's Ministry;* John Line, *The Doctrine of the Christian Ministry;* Robert S. Paul, *Ministry.)*

3. T. W. Manson, *The Church's Ministry* (Philadelphia: The Westminster Press, 1948), p. 91.

4. John Line, *The Doctrine of the Christian Ministry* (Toronto: The Ryerson Press, 1959), p. 124.

5. *Ibid.*, p. 129.

6. *Ibid.*, p. 130.

7. Robert McAfee Brown, *The Spirit of Protestantism* (New York: Oxford University Press, 1965), pp. 94–117.

8. Hendrik Kraemer, *The Theology of the Laity* (Philadelphia: The Westminster Press, 1958), p. 136.

9. John Calvin, *Corpus Reformatorum*, 51, 196. Also Wilhelm Niesel, *The Theology of Calvin*, trans. Harold Knight (Philadelphia: The Westminster Press, 1956), p. 202.

10. Charles Hodge, *What Is Presbyterianism?* (Philadelphia: Presbyterian Board of Publication, 1855), p. 36.

11. *Ibid.*, pp. 36–37.

12. John Calvin, *Institutes, IV:* 3, 3. Also Niesel, *op.cit.*, p. 203.

13. Robert S. Paul, *Ministry*, (Grand Rapids: William B. Eerdmans, 1965), pp. 133–142; 144–146.

14. Harry G. Goodykoontz, *The Minister in the Reformed Tradition* (Richmond: John Knox Press, 1963), p. 116.

15. Line, *The Doctrine of the Christian Ministry*, p. 134.

16. J. M. Barkley, "Ordination" in *A Dictionary of Liturgy and Worship* (New York: Macmillan Co., 1972), pp. 296–7.

17. Line, *The Doctrine of the Christian Ministry*, p. 133.

18. Manson, *The Church's Ministry*, p. 102.

19. Line, *The Doctrine of the Christian Ministry*, p. 148.

20. Forsyth, *The Church and Its Sacraments*, p. 53.

BIBLIOGRAPHY OF BOOKS
AND ARTICLES QUOTED

Abba, Raymond. *Principles of Christian Worship.* New York: Oxford University Press, 1960.

Arndt, Elmer J. F. *The Font and the Table.* Ecumenical Studies in Worship, No. 16. Richmond: John Knox Press, 1967.

Baillie, Donald M. *The Theology of the Sacraments.* New York: Charles Scribner's Sons, 1957.

Barclay, William. *The Lord's Supper.* London: SCM Press, 1967.

Barkley, John M. *The Worship of the Reformed Church.* Ecumenical Studies in Worship, No. 15. Richmond: John Knox Press, 1967.

Benoit, J. D. *Liturgical Renewal.* London: SCM Press, 1958.

Brenner, Scott Francis. *The Art of Worship.* New York: The Macmillan Co., 1961.

Brink, Frederick W. *This Man and This Woman.* New York: Association Press, 1948.

Bruce, Robert. *The Mystery of the Lord's Supper.* Translated and edited by Thomas F. Torrance. Richmond: John Knox Press, 1958.

Brunner, Emil. *The Divine-Human Encounter.* Philadelphia: The Westminster Press, 1943.

Cailliet, Emile, and Blankenagel, John. *Great Shorter Works of Pascal.* Philadelphia: The Westminster Press, 1948.

Calvin, John. *Institutes of the Christian Religion.* Translated by Henry Beveridge. Grand Rapids: W. B. Eerdmans, 1953.

Coffin, Henry Sloane. *The Public Worship of God.* Philadelphia: The Westminster Press, 1946.

Cope, G. F., Davies, J. G., and Tytler, D. A. *An Experimental Liturgy.* Richmond: John Knox Press, 1958.

Cope, Gilbert (ed.). *Making the Building Serve the Liturgy.* London: A. R. Mowbray, 1962.

Constantine. "State Recognition of Sunday, 321." *Documents of the Christian Church*. Edited by Henry Bettenson. New York: Oxford University Press, 1947.

Cullmann, Oscar. *Early Christian Worship*. Studies in Biblical Theology, No. 10. Chicago: Henry Regnery Co., 1953.

Davies, Horton M. *Christian Worship: Its History and Meaning*. Nashville: Abingdon Press, 1957.

Debuyst, Frédéric. *Modern Architecture and Christian Celebration*. Ecumenical Studies in Worship, No. 18. Richmond: John Knox Press, 1968.

Detlie, J. S. "A Religious Architecture for Today." *Religious Buildings for Today*. New York: Dodge, 1937,

Dix, Dom Gregory. *The Shape of the Liturgy*. Westminster, England: Dacre Press, 1949.

Doumergue, E. *Jean Calvin*. Lausanne: G. Bridel, 1902.

Dow, John. *This Is Our Faith*. Toronto: United Church Publishing House, 1943.

Flemington, W. F. *The New Testament Doctrine of Baptism*. London: SPCK, 1948.

Foreman, Kenneth J. *From This Day Forward*. Richmond: Outlook Publishers, 1950.

Forsyth, P. T. *The Church and the Sacraments*. London: Independent Press, 1947.

Forsyth, P. T. *Positive Preaching and the Modern Mind*. London: Hodder & Stoughton, 1949.

Hageman, Howard. *Pulpit and Table*. Richmond: John Knox Press, 1962.

Hahn, Ferdinand. *The Worship of the Early Church*. Translated by D. E. Green. Introduction by J. Reumann. Philadelphia: Fortress Press, 1973.

Hardin, H. Graydon, Quillian, Joseph D., and White, James F. *The Celebration of the Gospel*. Nashville: Abingdon Press, 1964.

Hauck, Allan. *Calendar of Christianity*. New York: Association Press, 1961.

Hedley, George. *Christian Worship*. New York: The Macmillan Co., 1953.

Heimsath, Charles H. *The Genius of Public Worship*. New York: Charles Scribner's Sons, 1947.

Hendry, George S. *The Westminster Confession for Today*. Richmond: John Knox Press, 1960.

Hislop, D. H. *Our Heritage in Public Worship*. Edinburgh: T. & T. Clark, 1936.

Hunter, A. Mitchell. *The Teaching of Calvin*. London: James Clark & Co., 1950.

Huxtable, John. *The Bible Says*. Richmond: John Knox Press, 1962.

Jeremias, Joachim. *The Eucharistic Words of Jesus*. New York: The Macmillan Co., 1955.

Jones, C., Wainwright, E., & Yarnold, E. (ed.). *The Study of Liturgy*. New York: Oxford University Press, 1978.

Keir, T. H. *The Word in Worship*. New York: Oxford University Press, 1962.

Kerr, Hugh Thompson. *The Christian Sacraments*. Philadelphia: The Westminster Press, 1944.

Kettring, Donald D. *Steps Toward a Singing Church*. Philadelphia: The Westminster Press, 1948.

Lake, Kirsopp (ed.). *The Apostolic Fathers*. Cambridge: Harvard University Press, 1959.

Lockett, William. *The Architectural Setting of the Liturgy*. London: SPCK, 1964.

Lovelace, Austin C., and Rice, William C. *Music and Worship in the Church*. Nashville: Abingdon Press, 1960.

Lüthi, Walter, and Thurneysen, Eduard. *Preaching, Confession, the Lord's Supper*. Richmond: John Knox Press, 1960.

Maxwell, William D. *Concerning Worship*. London: Oxford University Press, 1948.

Maxwell, William D. *An Outline of Christian Worship*. New York: Oxford University Press, 1958.

McArthur, A. Allan. *The Christian Year and Lectionary Reform*. London: SCM Press, 1958.

McArthur, A. Allan, *The Evolution of the Christian Year*. London: SCM Press, 1953.

McCabe, Joseph E. *The Power of God in a Parish Program*. Philadelphia: The Westminster Press, 1959.

McCabe, Joseph E. *Service Book for Ministers*. New York: McGraw-Hill Book Co., 1961.

McMillan, William. *The Worship of the Scottish Reformed Church: 1550 –1638*. Edinburgh: Lassodie Press, 1931.

Micklem, Nathaniel (ed.). *Christian Worship*. New York: Oxford University Press, 1936.

Micklem, Nathaniel. *Congregationalism and the Church Catholic*. London: Independent Press, 1944.

Milligan, Oswald. *The Ministry of Worship*. London: Oxford University Press, 1941.

Nichols, J. H., and Trinterud, L. J. *The Architectural Setting for Reformed Worship*. Presbytery of Chicago, 1960.

Nichols, James H. *Corporate Worship in the Reformed Tradition.* Philadelphia: The Westminster Press, 1968.
Niesel, Wilhelm. *The Theology of Calvin.* Philadelphia: The Westminster Press, 1956.
Paquier, Richard. *Dynamics of Worship.* Translation of Traité de Liturgique, by Donald Macleod. Philadelphia: Fortress Press, 1967.
Paul, Robert S. *Ministry.* Grand Rapids: William B. Eerdmans, 1965.
Pliny. *Letters,* II. Edited by W. M. L. Hutchison. New York: Macmillan & Co., 1915.
Reed, Luther. *Worship.* Philadelphia: Fortress Press, 1959.
Schuette, Walter E. *The Minister's Personal Guide.* New York: Harper & Brothers, 1953.
Schweizer, Eduard. *The Lord's Supper According to the New Testament.* Philadelphia: Fortress Press, Facet Books, 1967.
Sclater, J. R. P. *The Public Worship of God.* New York: George H. Doran Co., 1927.
Shands, Alfred R. *The Liturgical Movement and the Local Church.* London: SCM Press, 1959.
Shepherd, Massey H., Jr. (ed.). *The Liturgical Renewal of the Church.* New York: Oxford University Press, 1960.
Sovik, Edward A. *Architecture for Worship.* Minneapolis: Augsburg Publishing House, 1973.
Sperry, Willard L. *Reality in Worship.* New York: The Macmillan Co., 1925.
Temple, William. *The Hope of a New World.* New York: The Macmillan Co., 1942.
Thompson, Bard. *Liturgies of the Western Church.* Cleveland, Ohio: The World Publishing Co., 1961.
Vaughan, H. W. (ed.). *The Living Church.* Toronto: Ryerson Press, 1949.
von Allmen, Jean-Jacques. *Preaching and Congregation.* Ecumenical Studies in Worship, No. 10. Richmond: John Knox Press, 1962.
von Allmen, Jean-Jacques. *The Lord's Supper.* Ecumenical Studies in Worship, No. 19. Richmond: John Knox Press, 1969.
Wallace, Ronald S. *Calvin's Doctrine of the Word and Sacrament.* Edinburgh: Oliver & Boyd, 1953.
Whale, J. S. *Christian Doctrine.* New York: Cambridge University Press, 1963.
Williams, J. G. *Worship and the Modern Child.* London: SPCK, 1957.
Wilson, F. E. *An Outline of the Christian Year.* New York: Morehouse-Gorham Co., 1960.

ARTICLES

DATE DUE

Barr, James. "Further[.?] ... [2 1984] ... [ ] ... ! of Theology. Vol. IV, No. 3, pp.

Burkhart, Roy. "The Service of Memory." ... Vol. I, No. 5, pp. 22–27.

Davidson, Richard. "The Worship of the Reformed Churches." *The Presbyterian Register.* Vol. XVII, No. 10, pp. 292–296.

Howe, Reuel. "Overcoming Barriers to Communication." *The Princeton Seminary Bulletin.* Vol. LVI, No. 3, pp. 44–52.

Jacobs, Paul. "The Holy Spirit and the Development of Thought in the Modern Period Down to Existentialism." *The Reformed and Presbyterian World.* Vol. XXVII, No. 2, pp. 60–67.

Schweizer, Eduard. "Worship in the New Testament." *The Reformed and Presbyterian World.* Vol. XXIV, No. 5, pp. 196–205.

Thurneysen, Eduard. "The Biblical and Dogmatic Foundation of Pastoral Theology." *The Reformed and Presbyterian World.* Vol. XXV, No. 3, pp. 108–114.

Vajta, Vilmos. "The Theological Basis and Nature of the Liturgy." *Lutheran World.* Vol. VI, No. 3, pp. 234–246.

Zuch, Lowell H. "The Changing Meaning of the Funeral in Christian History." *Pastoral Psychology.* Vol. VIII, No. 78, pp. 17–26.